Young Children's Rights

Children in Charge series
Editor: Mary John
The series concentrates on the theme of children's rights, reflecting the increasing knowledge and research activity in this area. The perspectives of empowerment and of 'voice' run through the series, and the United Nations' Convention on the Rights of the Child is used as a benchmark. The series editor, Mary John, a developmental psychologist by training, is visiting professor at the University of Exeter. Her research and policy advisory work has been with minority rights groups. Her techniques in this work with marginalised groups have ensured that the research itself is a process of social change and individual empowerment.

Children's Rights in Education
Edited by Stuart Hart, Cynthia Price Cohen, Martha Farrell Erickson and Malfrid Flekkøy
ISBN 1 85302 977 7
Children in Charge 11

Traveller Children
A Voice for Themselves
Cathy Kiddle
ISBN 1 85302 684 0
Children in Charge 8

Education Citizenship and Independent Learning
Rhys Griffith
ISBN 1 85302 611 5
Children in Charge 6

Children as Citizens
Education for Participation
Edited by Cathie Holden and Nick Clough
ISBN 1 85302 566 6
Children in Charge 5

The Participation Rights of the Child
Rights and Responsibilities in Family and Society
Målfrid Grude Flekkøy and Natalie Hevener Kaufman
ISBN 1 85302 489 9 hb
ISBN 1 85302 490 2 pb
Children in Charge 4

A Charge Against Society
The Child's Right to Protection
Edited by Mary John
ISBN 1 85302 411 2
Children in Charge 3

Children in Our Charge
The Child's Right to Resources
Edited by Mary John
ISBN 1 85302 369 8
Children in Charge 2

Children in Charge
The Child's Right to a Fair Hearing
Edited by Mary John
ISBN 1 85302 368 X
Children in Charge 1

Children in Charge 10

Young Children's Rights

Exploring Beliefs, Principles and Practice

Priscilla Alderson

Forewords by
Save the Children and Mary John

Jessica Kingsley Publishers
London and Philadelphia

First published in the United Kingdom in 2000 by
Jessica Kingsley Publishers Ltd,
116 Pentonville Road,
London N1 9JB, England
and
325 Chestnut Street,
Philadelphia, PA 19106, USA.

www.jkp.com

Copyright © 2000 Priscilla Alderson

Second impression 2001

Library of Congress Cataloging in Publication Data
Alderson, Priscilla
    Young children's rights: exploring beliefs, attitudes, principles
and practice / Priscilla Alderson.
        p. cm. -- (Children in Charge ; 10)
    Includes bibliographical references.
    ISBN 1-85302-880- (pbk. : alk. paper)
    1. Children's rights. 2. Children and adults. 3. Interpersonal
communication. I. Title. II. Children in charge series ; 10.
HQ789 .A618 2000
305.23--dc21
                                                            99-056736

British Library Cataloguing in Publication Data
A CIP catalogue record for this book is available from the British Library

ISBN 1 85302 880 0

Printed and Bound in Great Britain by
Athenaeum Press, Gateshead, Tyne and Wear

Contents

Foreword

Save the Children is the UK's leading international children's charity, working to create a better future for children. We are committed to working towards enabling all children to have a happy, healthy and secure childhood. In a world where children are denied basic human rights, we are also exploring with children ways of realising children's rights in all the contexts within which children live.

Children's rights remain an area of contention for many, despite the fact that the United Nations Convention on Rights of the Child 1989 is the most widely ratified international human rights instrument. In the UK, the debate continues. Do children have any right to express their views about their contact with their parents, if their parents are separated, for example? There is opposition to the extension of rights, and even more so when we consider the rights of the youngest children, those under the age of eight. The idea that young children can think, comment and participate in any useful way is deemed by many commentators to be at best misguided and at worst a direct attack on the rights of the family.

For generations, children in many societies have been conceptualised as little more than empty vessels, with irrational needs and wants that have to be thwarted and tamed, all for the good of society. But as adults we face choices about how we perceive and react to children.

Save the Children has been interested in exploring the real implications and ethical considerations as well as the practice of truly working to a rights agenda in relation to the youngest children. We were delighted when Priscilla Alderson agreed to work with us on this daunting yet essential task of trying to articulate the arguments for young children's participation, from an adult perspective. She has posed the arguments in ways that require the reader to take on the full implications of a thoroughgoing commitment to young children's rights.

Our argument is that if concerns about citizenship and democracy are to be tackled effectively then we must recognise the human rights of all our citizens, including the youngest. We believe that this book is an important contribution to current thinking, and a practical resource for everyone who is concerned with making children's rights a reality.

Younger Children's Team,
Save the Children, London

Foreword

It is exciting to have as part of the Children in Charge Series this book which focuses on young children, examining values which colour interactions, frameworks which influence interventions with them and the nature of those practices themselves. Work with young children, whilst a much neglected area, is a vital part of the realisation of children's rights and understanding the necessary renegotiation of the adult-child relationships that are the core of respecting young children's agency and personal powers in a changing world. In these negotiations the voice of the child has to be heard and understood. Who better to take us through such work than Priscilla Alderson who has long been regarded as an expert in this field? The examples she provides in this important book serve to redress some of the imbalance in the literature on children's rights which is sorely limited when the critical gaze falls on very young children. This 'blind spot' is in itself interesting as children are often said to be 'not yet' adults and have therefore traditionally often been marginalised and ignored. Ironically within the literature on children's rights it has also often seemed that infants and young children are 'not yet' even children and therefore in disciplines and practices that should be concerned to protect their important place as people and citizens they have yet again been overlooked.

The Children in Charge Series in its accumulating volumes has brought together accounts of activities going on around the world. Thes relate to the realisation and execution of the aims of the United Nations Convention on the Rights of the Child. In November 1999 it was the 10th anniversary of the signing of that Convention so tracking the achievements during this first decade has been particularly important in raising awareness of the full implications of this legally binding instrument. Jessica Kingsley Publishers, I am proud to say, appreciated early how significant this would be. The Series was named 'Children in Charge' rather than Children's Rights quite deliberately to emphasise the stance adopted throughout. The present volume provides a particularly good example of this in providing detailed practical illustrations of the ways in which even young children are significant actors and potentially powerful agents in shaping the relationships and societies in which they live.

The Series so far has looked in detail at elements in the processes by which children claim and exercise their rights. This was approached in an interdisciplinary, multicultural way by the papers in the first three volumes which sprang from our early exploratory World Conference at Exeter in 1992 on this theme in the Convention. This was a significant event in that it was the first international conference in which young people were crucially involved. In the initial volumes the implications of the United Nations Convention in practical, theoretical and research terms were teased out, aided by the arguments, participation and inside knowledge of our Young People's Evaluation Panel. Those volumes (*Children in Charge, Children in Our Charge, A Charge Against Society*) crystallised around the 'three P's' by which the various Articles of the Convention are traditionally grouped – Provision, Protection and Participation. It is the realisation of the last of these three that has been the most challenging aspect of implementation of the Convention being addressed but warily by many practitioners, researchers and policy makers around the world. In recent times there has been a burgeoning literature on children's participation. Few of these works, however, have provided material on the participation of infants and young children and how this may be facilitated and encouraged. In this context, therefore, it is particularly pleasing to be led across this potential minefield so skilfully and with such clarity as Priscilla Alderson does in this present volume. It demonstrates how infants and young children can be realistically involved in choices and decisions such that their specific views and aspirations are translated and incorporated into the practices of the various institutions of their world. Both practical and theoretical issues are addressed and some of the established academic 'wisdom' which she argues has been misleading is fearlessly interrogated. 'Developmentalism', for instance, which has offered excuses in terms of the development of 'competencies' for not involving children until they are older and 'more competent', comes under close scrutiny.

Priscilla Alderson has published widely, largely so far in the 'grey' literature on children's rights. She is not only very well known as a hands-on researcher and practitioner but highly respected by academics and practitioners alike. Her monograph for Barnardo's on *Listening to Children: Children, Ethics and Social Research* (1995) provided one of the best pieces of writing, thinking and guidance in this area. Work on changing our school in collaboration with Highfield school pupils provided a contribution based in real effective practice to the increase of interest in children's participation (1997). The present book makes an original and thoughtful addition to the literature in a particularly sparse area on the participation of very young children. Such a focus has been avoided by many academics. This has been partly because it is such a challenging area in which to work. It requires consummate skill and inventiveness on the part of the researcher, endless patience, a certain empathy and understanding that can only come with long years of working with children rather than on them. Material presented here is deceptively simple yet has been the product of tireless research, collecting, sifting and archiving. A vast array of material from the UK is scanned and assembled around the ongoing argument such that it is readable for the uninitiated and challenging to professional insiders. I would argue that such data form the very cornerstone of any further understanding of the participation of young children.

The research and writing of Priscilla Alderson have been a significant influence in the field of childhood studies particularly in the area of the active involvement of children. This latest contribution will ensure that views of adults about the pervasive powerlessness of young children will be challenged. The capabilities of the young children here portrayed will astonish and, hopefully, the nature of the relationships between adults and young children will start to change as they have to if these young people are to set out appropriately empowered to take charge of their lives and to share in the charge to transform the world of tomorrow which is theirs.

Mary John
Series Editor

REFERENCES

Alderson, P. (1995) *Listening to Children: Children, Ethics and Social Research.* Barkinside, Barnardos.

Alderson, P. (1997) *Changing our School: Promoting Positive Behaviour.* Plymouth: Highfield School/London. Institute of Education.

Acknowledgements

I am grateful to Save the Children and especially Nicky Road for planning this book and commissioning me to write it, and for the generous help of the advisory group, although I am responsible for any shortcomings and for some views expressed here. The advisory group members who, with many other colleagues, provided too many examples of active young children to include all of them in this book, are: Nicky Road, Chris Cuninghame, Sue Emerson, Lina Fajerman, Tina Hyder and Bharti Mepani of Save the Children; Gerison Lansdown, Director of the Children's Rights Office; Judith Stone, until recently Chief Executive of the National Early Years Network; Judy Miller, a Child Care Consultant; and Carolyne Willow, who is employed by Article 12, the national organisation run for and by children and young people. I would also like to thank all the children and adults whose views and experiences have contributed to this book, Dorothy Judd for giving permission for the picture in Chapter 8 to be reprinted, and Mary John, Helen Parry, Dorothy Clift, Jackie Lee and Linda Attwell for help with editing.

Introduction

CHILDREN'S RIGHTS

'We hear far too much about children's rights' is a frequently-made assertion. It is often stated in response to examples of children appearing to be greedy, selfish and irresponsible, demanding anything from holidays in Florida to designer trainers. Yet these luxuries have little to do with children's rights.

The difference between luxuries and rights is illustrated, for example, by media stories during the school holidays of parents having to ferry children around from one expensive treat to the next – swimming pools, sports and music sessions, zoos and theme parks. These outings are very enjoyable but, when asked what they most enjoy, children tend to say 'time with my friends', 'playing games in the park', 'messing about on the beach or by the river', 'taking my dog for a walk'. These answers are closer to basic human rights: freedom to enjoy and move around the area where they live, to meet their friends and be members of their local community, to enjoy nature, to play actively and creatively rather than be passive consumers.

Many children are denied these simple freedoms because of dangerous traffic and undue fear of strangers exacerbated by media panics, because crowded built-up areas have no safe, clean, outdoor spaces to play, and so much of the countryside is fenced-off as private property. As a result, young children usually have to rely on busy adults to escort them into the street or to arrange to meet a friend. They are virtually imprisoned in their own homes in Britain.

For families without large-enough gardens, the easiest way to enjoy being outside with friends is to go on an outing, to pay for access to pools, or woods, or animals, or space to play sports. Over the past few decades, the closing down of public spaces to children (even school grounds are locked up during the holidays) and the opening up of commercial services to replace the free public ones have made children's ability to exercise basic rights seem like luxuries. Compare British childhoods today with those a few decades ago, such as Laurie Lee's childhood in Gloucestershire (Lee 1959).

It is adults, however, who have effected this commercial transformation, including the pressures from advertising. It is therefore illogical and ironic to blame children for this change, and to see their requests for simple rights, such as to meet their friends, as greedy irresponsible demands. A further irony is that children are often asking to do what health promoters exhort people to do, to take more exercise and spend time with friends. Yet when children cannot run about or ride bikes near their homes, their chances to be active have to be turned into special outings arranged by adults. Town planning and other pressures make young children much more dependent on adults than they actually need to be, as later examples will show, so that again it is ironic to blame children for their enforced dependence and to call it being lazy or irresponsible. Thus, claims that 'we hear too much about children's rights' raise questions about which rights are being referred to, and are they really rights? One aim of this book is to define the different types of children's rights and to review how much they are respected in the UK towards the next century.

CAN AND SHOULD YOUNG CHILDREN BE ASKED TO GIVE THEIR VIEWS IN MATTERS WHICH AFFECT THEM?

These are the key questions for this book. Early drafts began with titles such as *Consulting Young Children* or *Listening to Young Children*. Gradually the adult-centredness of such titles became clearer. They imply active adults taking the lead, setting the agenda and starting the interactions, while children more passively follow and respond – or do not respond.

Children and adults communicating is the main theme of this book, though often in the form of questions about how it is possible or worthwhile, wise or kind, for adults to consult and involve the youngest children. However, the answers challenge the questions by including examples of babies sometimes leading the way, which makes this book an appropriate inclusion in Jessica Kingsley's *Children in Charge* Series. One aim in this book is partly to untangle common perceptions about young children from direct examples of their own words and activities.

Another aim is to show how very early young children can share in complex activities.

The United Nations Convention on the Rights of the Child (UN 1989), Article 12, says that States shall assure 'to the child who is capable of forming his or her own views the right to express those views freely in all matters affecting the child'. The Children Act of England and Wales (DoH 1989) says: 'Have regard in particular to the ascertainable wishes and feelings of the child concerned.' Yet do these policies help or harm children and adults? To begin with, here are examples of young children expressing their views, taken from growing numbers of reports on this topic.

The Kids Council in Everton first began by running a disco. All young people in the area from the age of two years and over could be a member, until the minimum age was raised to eight years in 1993. They meet monthly and employed a children's worker from 1993. They are concerned about conditions for old people, for whom they run popular bingo sessions, as well as being concerned about children and teenagers. Half the houses on the estate are empty and vandalised, and the Kid's Council has advised the local authority about which houses to restore and about traffic calming methods, as well as sharing in street clean-ups and the local gala. They spend time talking about how to learn from their achievements and mistakes, one of their main aims (Save the Children 1997c).

Tackling bullying

At one school, seven-year-olds suggested conducting a survey about bullying. Bullying is so often discussed in terms of *who* bullies *whom*. Instead, they went round the school asking *where* and *when* were people most likely to be bullied. Certain areas of the play ground were often cited. As a result of the survey of the children's own knowledge, lunch-time supervisors spread out around the play ground and near to these areas, and there was far less bullying (Rowe 1999).

Replanning a housing estate

When a run-down housing estate was being renovated, the adults were consulted but not, at first, the children. Then children aged from three to eight years began to be asked about the new plans, and about what they enjoyed or would like to have on the estate. This started almost by chance – initially the adults were surprised by the children's clear views, and worked step-by-step with the children about how to involve them. 'I've done a lot of work with children in this age group,' said the Children Should be Heard project worker, Brian Wood. 'But it was a huge leap from working as someone who was providing a service to recognising that children actually have views on services and issues where they live.'

His first questions did not gain many replies, so he asked the children to show him around the estate as a newcomer, and to take photographs of things that were important to them. Ten children joined in the tour, showing a heap of sand, a stream and a bridge they had made. Eventually the children wrote a report, illustrating it with their drawings, maps, photos, and including details of their survey of other children's views. They discussed the report with senior council officers. A play area had been planned for them beyond the perimeter road. On their advice it was sited instead in the centre of the estate away from traffic and passing strangers, and where the children could safely arrive and play without needing their parents to be with them (Newson 1995a).

School councils

Every school in Richmond, Surrey has a school council and members from each school also meet regularly in borough-wide meetings. They share their concerns and choose four main topics each term to discuss with local councillors. Primary-school members have asked, for example, how they can help homeless people in Richmond. Each term they raise their four new topics, and also hear councillors' reports on action taken on previous concerns.

Attitudes in schools about children's meetings when teachers are not present

- Some primary schools encourage children to arrange their own meetings, such as a music or drama group, or meetings for school captains or for peer mediators (Highfield School 1997). The teachers believe it is important to encourage the children to be responsible, and to have time and space to work out their own ideas and activities.

- In contrast, one secondary school senior teacher, speaking of people aged 11 to 18, said that at her school: 'We would like to do things like that, but the children cannot be allowed to hold meetings without staff present. Someone might flick a paper clip into someone's eye, and it could get into the newspapers. Parents would stop sending their children to this school, and I would have to sack some of the teachers. Everyone would suffer, and we just cannot afford to take this kind of risk. It is all for their own good that we do not let the children have this kind of meeting.'

JOINING IN

Monika Riihelda has pioneered Storyride, in which adults listen intently to young children's stories, write them down and read them back to the child (Riihelda 1996). Among the reported benefits are the adults' and children's enjoyment and new habits of listening more carefully to one another. Storyride is becoming an international network, and one four-year-old has told over 700 stories. Asked the age at which she believes children can begin to be consulted, Monika Riihelda replied 'eight months' and gave the following example.

Five Finnish children aged up to five years sat round a table and each child in turn told a story which the adult wrote down and read back. Finally all the children turned to look at the baby at the end of the row who was watching. He made noises and was clearly pleased when the adult wrote them down and read them back.

Monika added:

'But I think the principle is, that every human being has stories to be told, if there is somebody who has the interest to listen to them. So it does not depend on the age of the teller, but on the sensitivity of the listener. A newborn baby is looking in your eyes, making silent questions, asking for cooperation, for building a common world. That is one of the beginnings of the stories.'

The baby had grasped some of the essentials. He wanted to take part with the others and be listened to, despite not completely understanding. When adults make major decisions they cannot necessarily understand and foresee all that is involved. The key questions, when consulting adults or children, rather than 'Do they either understand or not?' are 'Do they understand enough? And, if not, could they understand enough if they had more information, or if they were asked in different ways?' Children's decisions are often about wanting to take a fuller part and a greater responsibility in activities which they see others doing. The housing estate and anti-bullying examples show how children have unique knowledge about solutions which can very much benefit children and adults.

THE READERS

This book is written for a wide range of people: those who work closely with young children and others who spend more time in management and policy-making; people who want to extend the ways they already consult children and those who have not yet consulted them much.

The book is also for people from a range of backgrounds: play and education; health and social services; and other local government and voluntary services – for practitioners and students and their tutors. Parents may find this book useful in their relationships with their own children, and when they want to encourage other adults, such as teachers or town planners, to listen to children. Examples will be given of children talking, for instance, about play or health care, to make points about children's general understanding and abilities, which readers from other disciplines can apply to their work.

WHO SHOULD CONSULT YOUNG CHILDREN?

Clear communication is vital when adults consult children about care and services provided for them, and about involving children as more active partners in caring for themselves and for one another. Are visiting researchers more useful than adults who know the children well, but who may doubt they have the skill or time to consult children? Researchers report that after they know a group of young children well, and a new researcher arrives, some children become quieter and take time to get used to the new person. Familiarity is important. Working in small close groups and taking time for the children to become used to the consulter also help to draw out fuller responses from the children. Rapport grows through enjoying shared experiences and through playful methods of enquiry. A useful involvement of outside expert researchers is demonstrated when they work with the staff until the staff take over doing the consulting routinely, convinced and confident that this is a worthwhile use of their time, as in the Redbridge study described later (National Early Years Network (NEYN) 1998). This is a more efficient use of outside advisers than to work as if children can only be consulted when experts are called in, leaving the staff and children less confident and more distant from one another.

PRACTICAL IDEAS

This book is mainly about *ideas* on children and adults communicating and consulting, for three reasons. First, powerful hidden ideas and assumptions lead people to want to begin or to block communication. These ideas need to be discussed openly so that their impact is understood, including older and newer ideas about childhood. Second, rather than duplicating the excellent practical books which have already been published, this book describes a few of their working examples and refers readers to them. Third, consulting children involves taking a fresh approach to *their* ideas including how to talk and listen to them. It involves sometimes following their leads, and relying less on methods that other adults have used. This book is not like a recipe book or a music score which are blueprints for reproducing predictable food or sounds. Instead, it is more about creating an understanding which will help adults and children to create their own methods, and perhaps to become more aware of ways they are already communicating. Talking and inventing, watching and listening are the keys, with confidence in one's own ideas and in the ideas of older and younger colleagues.

SAVE THE CHILDREN POLICY

National and international voluntary organisations for children take the 1989 UN Convention on the Rights of the Child very seriously, especially Article 12 on the child's right to express a view in all matters affecting the child. This book grew out of Save the Children staff's concerns about how to listen to and involve the youngest children. Some of Save the Children's policy is summarised here in order to explain the background thinking behind the writing of this book, and this could also be useful to readers who are thinking how to base their policies and practices on respect for young children.

The 1997 Global programme strategy (Save the Children 1997a, pp.10,14–20) states that Save the Children aims to be a catalyst, stimulating and encouraging changes and the structures to support them, and involving the people concerned, including young children, in this work. This includes responding to local social factors and agencies, and publicising the lessons learned from these powerful experiences.

Save the Children aims to:

- develop a programme of practical action from which to argue forcefully for children's rights, needs, interests and views to be placed at the centre of development across the world
- combat through its work the damage caused to children by policies, attitudes and actions which threaten their survival and development
- promote inclusive models of social and economic change which promote social justice and challenge all forms of discrimination
- be an effective witness, alongside our partners and children themselves, to the successes and failures of societies, North and South, to act responsibly towards children and safeguard their rights
- encourage recognition of children's active contribution – economic, social, cultural, and children's rights to be included and participate in their development
- work alongside policy-makers, practitioners and others to explore ways in which their decisions and actions can do more to realise children's rights and bring about long-term benefits for children.

To achieve these goals, Save the Children needs:

- to affirm the role of Save the Children's programmes in realising children's rights
- to secure the benefits of a more rigorous child-focused approach in Save the Children's own work
- to ensure lasting benefits for children through a range of approaches (such as partnership, capacity-building and participation) which support structures and organisations which can sustain work into the future

- to learn more effectively from experience and use it to generate support for the changes we seek through forceful advocacy and communication
- to establish clearer programme priorities and objectives, building competence in these areas.

New ways of listening to, and learning from, young children in different communities are crucial to these policies. Save the Children also aims to ensure that the reality of children's lives, especially of the most disadvantaged, informs all its work by:

- ensuring that whenever possible, children will share in identifying and validating issues and solutions (including more formal involvement in project design and review exercises) as well as in advocacy work
- building the capacity to work with children in a participatory way, by developing skills, tools, and methodologies which are sensitive to their ages, gender, culture and capabilities as well as to local views of childhood.

These policies raise many questions about how far they can possibly be fulfilled. One main question that is discussed in this book is: How much can or should babies and young children be involved in these processes?

BACKGROUND AND OUTLINE OF THE BOOK

This book draws on two main sources: many published reports of people's experiences and research, their reviews and ideas (references are given for these); and my own material – examples and ideas drawn from the playgroups and play schemes, children's homes, schools and hospitals where I have worked, from decades of living with young children, plus anecdotes by and about friends whose real names are not given, to protect their privacy. Some of the second sources are not referenced. Direct examples are used because so much of the literature about children and their rights and abilities, and about teaching and caring for them, is written at several removes from the daily reality of children's lives, and I wanted this book to reflect children's realities as much as possible.

This is not an original research report but a practical collection of ideas and examples, and a resource to help people to think about the main questions. Examples are not given to suggest that they are typical but to illustrate a point, and at times to expand notions of what a 'typical child' might be like. The subject is young children in the UK. No claims are made therefore that the subject is children everywhere, although a few examples come from other countries. It is important to remember that British children have too many mixed origins and backgrounds, and unknown potentials, to allow many generalisations about them.

Chapter 1 reviews young children's rights to be consulted within the framework of the United Nations Convention on the Rights of the Child, 1989, with its provision, protection and participation rights. Chapter 2 considers how young children are seen as people, human beings rather than human becomings, and explores the tensions between protecting children and respecting them. Standard beliefs and deeper feelings about whether young children can or should be consulted are reviewed in Chapter 3. Some confidence and trust on each side are needed, and these are affected by adults' and children's beliefs about childhood abilities. Chapter 4 looks at methods of listening to and working with young children, and Chapter 5 at two kinds of levels of doing so. One is their level or degree of involvement and participation, the other is the arena for involving them from small groups to international policies. Contradictions between notions of play and work when consulting children are considered in Chapter 6. Chapter 7 discusses further complications which discourage adults from consulting young children: worries about risk and control, conflict and violence. Relationships and interactions continue to be reviewed in Chapter 8, which examines children and adults working together and sharing some decisions, and responsibility for oneself and for others, as well as respecting and influencing one another's views and feelings, decisions and behaviour. Finally, the key messages from the evidence and experiences are summarised in Chapter 9. The notes and references are meant to be a resource for readers who would like to follow up topics raised in this book.

Writing this book has been a slow process because so many new ideas are scattered into so many places. Also, I kept finding that I was writing about what adults *do to* children, and my sentences needed rewriting so that children are also the actors. Sometimes, this continuing process feels like writing in a new language, which someone has compared with peeling away the layers of old thinking. It is quite easy with the dried, thin outer layers. Yet when going into the thicker living layers, the ones that are deeply part of everyday and partly subconscious life, it becomes much harder to be aware and willing to let go of old views of childhood and to try new ones.

CHAPTER ONE

Children's and Babies' Rights and the UN Convention on the Rights of the Child 1989

RIGHTS AND OBLIGATIONS

One of the main purposes of this book is to see how the United Nations 1989 Convention on the Rights of the Child applies to babies and the youngest of children and so, implicitly, to all other children. This chapter therefore reviews how the Convention defines and qualifies the three kinds of children's rights, with examples of how they affect children's daily lives.

The child's right to be consulted has gained new meaning through the Convention, by far the most widely-agreed international treaty, ratified by every government in the world except for Somalia which has no government and the US which does not ratify UN treaties. Ratification means that governments undertake to implement the Convention in law, policy and practice in its comprehensive 54 articles and to report regularly to the UN on their progress in doing so. The UK government reported in 1995 and will again in 2000 although the UN Committee on the Rights of the Child which receives and responds to the reports is behind with its work because of the unexpected and unprecedented number of governments involved.

The UK Government's 1995 response was received critically by the UN (UN 1995) and did not involve much consultation with people in Britain, although the Children's Rights Office published an immensely detailed report on the UK Government's (mainly lack of) progress in implementing the Convention (Lansdown and Newell 1994). The British Government's response prepared in 1999 involved wide consultation, carried out by Save the Children with 40 different groups of children and young people, many of whom have experiences and disadvantages which are linked to some aspects of the Convention. The

Children's Rights Office now has living web pages, frequently updated on the state of children's rights in the UK.

The UN 1989 Convention's formally-agreed standards cover: provision rights (to necessary, not luxury, goods, services and resources); protection rights (from neglect, abuse, exploitation and discrimination); and participation rights, when children are respected as active members of their family, community and society, as contributors from their first years.

Rights are *limited*. As legal concepts they concern freedoms and obligations which can be deliberately honoured or withheld. Parents cannot be taken to court, for example, for not loving their child. It would be useless and cruel to prosecute a mother who is too depressed to love her baby. Love and happiness cannot be willed or enforced so they cannot be rights. Adults can, however, be prosecuted for gross neglect or abuse, and children do have the right to be protected from these. The Convention sets all possible standards which can be enforced to help adults to give loving care, and the Convention's preamble states the importance of every child living 'in an atmosphere of happiness, love and understanding'. However, the Convention outlines minimum standards, which may rise in future as the world's children come to be more respected.

Some rights are *aspirational*, not yet fully realisable, but only 'to the maximum extent of [each nation's] available resources'(4)[1]. Rights are not *absolute* but *conditional*, affected by the 'evolving capacities of the child', the 'responsibilities, rights and duties of parents'(5), 'the primary responsibility of the parents' (18), and the national law. 'The best interests of the child shall be a primary consideration'(3). Children's rights cannot be exercised in ways which would harm the child or other people. In exercising their rights, people must 'respect the rights and reputations of others', as well as 'national security and public order, health and morals' (13).

Rights are *shared*, being about solidarity, social justice and fair distribution, 'our' rights not 'my' rights. To claim a right acknowledges that everyone has an equal claim to it and so reaffirms the worth and dignity of every person. Children's rights are part of promoting 'social progress and better standards of life in larger freedom'. The preamble

1   Figures in brackets refer to the relevant article of the Convention.

states that the child 'needs special safeguards and care, including appropriate legal protection,' and the Convention begins 'in recognition
of the inherent dignity and of the equal and inalienable rights of all
members of the human family [as] the foundation of freedom, justice
and peace in the world'.

One argument against children's rights is that rights cannot be
bestowed. They can only apply to groups which understand and claim
and exercise rights for themselves, as some, though far from all, women
and black people have struggled to do. Yet the provision and protection
rights involve duties which adults owe to children, who did not ask to
be born and who are inevitably dependent at first. With the participation rights, although young children may not use rights language,
they repeatedly say they want adults to listen to them and take heed of
their views, for example, in the consultations with children conducted
in 1999 to inform the British Government's report to the UN Committee on the Rights of the Child (and also Lansdown and Newell
1994; Save the Children 1999).

It is also said that rights go with obligations and responsibilities, and
that children are irresponsible. Adults are responsible for ensuring that
many children's rights are respected, but children often want some participation rights so that they can share more responsibility with adults,
as the examples in the introduction showed (Verhellen 1994). The next
sections go through some articles in the Convention to show how
provision, protection and participation rights can help young children
and adults to enjoy more equal and mutually-rewarding relationships.

I. PROVIDING FOR YOUNG CHILDREN

Standards of care

All services for children 'shall conform with the standards established
by competent authorities, particularly in the areas of safety, health, in
the number and suitability of their staff as well as competent supervision' (3).

Standards can include, and be informed by, regular consulting with
parents and children who use the services. Parents are seen as the main
'consumers' of day care, yet they may be loath to express concerns. They
are often absent and thus uncertain about what exactly is going on.
They may worry that their child will be unpopular or victimised, or will
lose the child's place, or that the parents will be blamed for the child's

problems, if they make comments. Travellers, for example, may be seen as uncooperative if they stop their children from sharing in school outings for fear that they may have to collect the children in an emergency if the police suddenly evict the traveller family from their site (Kiddle 1999). However, parents are a vital source of information, in their own views and in helping their child's views to be heard more clearly. Authorities such as the Department for Education and Employment recognise this right: 'Parents and other carers, children and young people should be consulted about their needs and preferences and these should be taken into account in developing provision [in a partnership] directed to the diverse needs and aspirations of children locally' (DfEE 1998a).

Health care

The child has the right to 'the enjoyment of the highest attainable standard of health and to facilities for treatment of illness and rehabilitation of health' especially 'to diminish infant and child mortality' (24). State parties shall develop primary health care, and provide 'adequate nutritious foods and clean drinking water…appropriate pre- and postnatal health care for mothers…health education [including] basic knowledge of child health and nutrition, the advantages of breast feeding, hygiene, and environmental sanitation and the prevention of accidents…and family planning services' (24).

Babies as health workers

From their first weeks children share in their own health care. The baby is necessarily the most active partner in breast- or bottle-feeding. With breast-feeding, the baby creates the demand which builds up the supply, and success depends on responding to the baby's requests for frequent feeds at first.

After eating most of the foods they are offered, between 18 to 24 months, many babies begin to refuse unfamiliar food. There may be a useful reason for their caution about one year after weaning, which works well in societies with limited diets and where young children roam quite freely. The children accept all the familiar seasonal foods, and are unlikely to try strange food like poisonous berries (Leidloff 1976).

The tradition of assuming that young children are not yet rational is
challenged by the evidence:

> It is clear from the beginning that children have a driving
> motivation to become part of a meaningful world. They want
> roles. They want to have tasks, they want to share interests, they
> want to have possessions, they like being able to share things
> with other people, they like to be able to share purposes and
> functions (Trevarthen 1999).

Babies as partners

Very soon babies start to share in dressing, by holding their arms
flexibly to help to put on sleeves, instead of being like limp or
rigid dolls. From about 12 months, they assert their independence, for example, by refusing to wear a coat on a cold or wet day.
If they are consulted they soon learn to know when they need to
wear a coat, as long as they are not teased or punished when they
change their minds. Young children are very keen to feed themselves, initiate games and interactions, and to cooperate and help.
During their second year they become active in their own and
others' health care, when helping with cooking and cleaning.

A study of mothers' and health visitors' views of 20-month-old
children (Mayall 1993) found that the mothers tended to see the
children as real people, full members of the family. The health visitors,
even those who were mothers, tended to believe out-of-date texts about
young children's inabilities and their need to be controlled and stimu-
lated by adults. The professionals tended not to advise consulting
children. The mothers went beyond consulting, towards living in a kind
of partnership with the children. Mothers and health visitors believed
that adults must quite firmly control and protect children but, perhaps
subconsciously, they took rather different approaches. The mothers
were happier to negotiate and share control. They saw the benefits, for
them and for the children, in helping the children to become more
active and responsible. The health visitors tended to assume that adults'

power should be enforced clearly, through conflict if necessary, rather than through consulting and negotiating.

Babies as carers

A television programme in 1997 told the story of a single mother who was deaf and blind and the social workers who felt that her baby should live with another family. The film showed the six-month-old smiling, friendly baby watching the spoonful of food her mother lifted towards her and guiding it into her own mouth. As she grew older, a neighbour commented that at the age when babies usually drop and throw things on the floor, the baby did not do this as if she knew that this would be difficult for her mother.

Some toddlers offer help and comfort to other children who are in distress, whereas others seem indifferent and some, who have been abused, seem pleased when others are unhappy (Bråten 1996).

Sisterly love

This newspaper headline was about twins who were born eleven weeks early. Chelsea was soon well enough to go home and she visited Daniel regularly and lay next to him in his special care cot at a Newcastle hospital. The babies cuddled up together and a photograph showed Daniel curling his fingers around Chelsea's hand. Their parents were convinced that the twins missed each other, and that Chelsea gave Daniel strength to get better during his months in hospital (London Metro, 6.8.99).

Adults play key roles in helping babies to become responsible for their self-care, and to be adventurous yet cautious enough to avoid injuries (Mayall 1994a). This may involve waiting, a kind of silent consulting, sometimes while children test and decide whether to take a risk in climbing and balancing, and gradually to increase their strength and skilful mobility.

Review when looked after (meaning children in the care of the local authority)

Any child cared for by authorities has the right to 'periodic review of the treatment provided to the child and all other circumstances relevant to his or her placement' (25).

Children's views should be attended to carefully (Gardner 1989; Willow 1996; Masson, Harrison and Paviovic 1997). This right applies to disabled, sick and other children in long-term health or social services care, and from as early as possible, the young child's feelings should be considered. Joseph Rowntree Foundation publications offer many practical suggestions on consulting these children (Knight 1998; Cavet 1998; Morris 1998; Noyes 1999).

Standard of living

Every child has the right 'to a standard of living adequate for the child's physical, mental, spiritual and social development ... State parties ... within their means' shall assist families when in need with, for example, food, clothing and housing (27).

As the Government's current concern with social exclusion illustrates, poverty can exclude people, and silence them when it is harder for them to belong to groups which are involved, respected and heard. By the end of the twentieth century, one in three children were living in poverty in Britain (Wilkinson 1994; Hutton 1995; Roberts 1997; Sgritta 1997). Proposing paid employment for their parents as the main solution to poverty for children raises problems for babies' adequate standard of living, unless they have very good day care while their parents work.

Economics plays a vital part in how children are consulted and involved. A review of nurseries in Italy, Spain and England shows great differences in the quality of the play and relationships, between the nurseries in beautiful centres which are honoured in their community, and the low-budget ones in poorer districts (Penn 1997a). There are creative nurseries in both kinds of areas, but many factors make it harder for the disadvantaged ones to be like the highest standard nurseries. Early years centres reflect and express their political setting and the adults' sense, and so indirectly the children's sense, of how much children are citizens with a right to be consulted and respected

(Edwards, Gandini and Forman 1998; Dahlberg, Moss and Pence 1999).

Young children express themselves through 'hundreds of languages' – all kinds of drama, dance, story, art and music. With varied materials and the sensitive support of skilled adults, children create things which delight and amaze people, such as the travelling exhibition of work by children in Reggio Emilia, Italy (Edwards, Gandini and Forman 1998). The prosperous city is renowned for spending over 10 per cent of its budget on the education of the children aged from four months to six years.

Far less is spent per child on schools in England. Although this is impossible to measure precisely, in 1993 it was estimated that for every £100 spent on leisure activities for adults, the Department of National Heritage spent three pence on activities for children, one fifth of the population (Laing 1993, p.181). The resources are not easily enjoyed by children when they have great difficulty in reaching public places which they might enjoy. As one six-year-old pointed out: 'We need more bridges over the roads so we can get to the park' (Lansdown and Newell 1994, p. 13; and see NVCCP Charter 1992; Shier 1995).

Hundreds of English playgroups were closed in the years 1998–99, partly because of new funding systems which enable schools to admit four-year-olds. One, from numerous examples, illustrates the financial pressures. A playgroup in a small town gets little support from the council, which wants to hand over the large hut to the Army Training Corps (ATC). The town's local newspaper reported the playgroup's imminent closure, because it could not afford to repair the leaking roof, at the same time as announcing the playgroup's glowing OFSTED (Office for Standards in Education) report. The councillors appear to see the ATC as a means of economising, by preventing crime and vandalism through economically disciplining young men. Young children do not present an immediate crime threat, and are seen as their parents' and not the town's responsibility financially. Yet early years centres provide true crime prevention when they encourage children to know they belong to a loving small community, to have confidence in themselves and in other people, to value other people and their property through being valued and creative people themselves (Duffy 1998).

One county council paid large sums to send some of its staff to Reggio Emelia, and over £20,000 to bring the exhibition to its area.

Meanwhile, various services and support for young children's activities locally were closing for lack of small grants.

Education and cultural life

Primary education shall be 'compulsory and free to all' (28) and involves 'the preparation of the child for responsible life in a free society, in the spirit of understanding, peace, tolerance, equality of sexes, and friendship among all peoples' (29). Informal education in understanding and responsibility starts from birth and includes listening and responding to children's wishes. The child has the right 'to rest and leisure, to engage in play…and to participate freely in cultural life and the arts' (31).

Educational services for young children are expanding with school places for 4-year-olds and more educational support in child care services (DfEE 1998a). However, thousands of children are excluded from schools each year, including some 4-year-olds who could be seen to be in greatest need of care and appropriate education services (CRE 1996). Cultural life and the arts are crucial aspects of education and many details of daily life, such as children's food, clothes and housing, songs, games and language, express their culture and how much they are valued in their community. Playtrain aims to increase ways of listening to and involving children through play and the arts (Playtrain 1995; Cox 1997). One aim is to overcome barriers between the élitist professional art world and children's everyday lives, helping them to access high-quality painting and sculpture, theatre and music, museums and exhibitions. The arts are for everyone, enriching their lives inestimably and helping to reduce crime and alienation when, for example, people belong to music or drama groups. A further great gain is the innumerable beautiful and original works children create when they have the chance.

Children and adults appreciate moving, interactive and hands-on exhibits, pictures hung at their differing eye-levels, and smell and mirror boxes. Some galleries' new child-friendly policies have dramatically increased the numbers of enthusiastic young visitors, and are grounded in consultations with them. The booklets which many art galleries now provide, for children to search, for example, for insects in famous paintings, appeal to their excited curiosity and their satisfaction in filling in the answers, and are also very rewarding for adults (Pearce 1998).

Consulting through the arts

Children were involved as contributors when they designed large murals of a rainforest and a desert in Swansea art gallery, in projects which involved blind and other disabled children. They visited a wildlife park to touch the animals at the design stage. Children's creativity is inspired directly when they work with clay and paint during visits to exhibitions, or work with professional actors and dancers.

Far from being escapism, art enables children to develop and express their concerns and values. The Wheelworks mobile community arts programme in Belfast, for instance, helps them to transcend barriers when children from different communities work together.

The group *Children 2000*, working with children, aims to increase the profile of children at all levels of funding and planning in the arts, media, sports, leisure, education, environment, health and well-being, building and transport. They want all national lottery applications to have clauses on children's needs and equal rights, for all applicants and assessors to consider (Cox 1997).

Publicising the Convention

State parties undertake to make the principles of the Convention 'widely known, by appropriate and active means, to adults and children alike' (42).

The British Government has done comparatively little to publicise the Convention to children or to adults. Ideas from the expressive South African photograph posters, which show pictures of children with captions quoting articles from the Convention, could be copied in this country. Posters drawn by children can be displayed in health and early years settings as well as other public places to increase public awareness of children's rights (Save the Children 1999).

(II) PROTECTING YOUNG CHILDREN

Violence and neglect

States shall 'protect the child from all forms of physical or mental violence, injury or abuse, neglect or negligent treatment, maltreatment or exploitation' (19). Preventing physical punishment is another right which applies to babies especially as the most vulnerable people. In the UK, children are the only people who can, in law, be hit. Over 90 per cent of British babies are smacked (Newson and Newson 1990), and babies and the youngest children are hit the most often (Smith 1995; Leach 1999). Smacking does not prevent wrong doing (Miller 1983). Many adults think it is impossible to reason with young children: 'a smack is the only language they understand'. Consulting young children about their behaviour and about positive discipline, as soon as they begin to understand, is the way to avoid physical punishment (Newell 1989).

Smacking hurts you inside

A recent study of the views of 76 five to seven-year-old children's thoughtful views on smacking vividly reports the pain and fear they feel, and the many reasons for which children are hit (Willow and Hyder 1998). This can include, for example, being accidentally clumsy, so that for some children a smack seems to be an arbitrary, unpredictable adult response that could happen at any moment, not something which the child knows how to prevent. This is counterproductive if smacking is meant to be a deterrent. A few children said they felt so sad 'it makes you not like your parents' or 'you feel like you want to run away'.

The UK's record on Article 19 was one of the main criticisms in 1995 by the UN Committee on the Rights of the Child, which receives and comments from regular reports from all the governments (UN 1995). Yet since then, although physical punishment in private schools is now banned, the courts have expanded adults' rights to hit children to child minders when parents authorise them to do so.

Respect for cultural background

Children temporarily deprived of their family environment 'shall be entitled to special protection and assistance provided by the State' (20). In cases of adoption and other alternative care, 'due regard shall be paid to the desirability of continuity in a child's upbringing and to the child's ethnic, religious, cultural and linguistic background' (20).

This right is also important in all settings where babies and young children are cared for, partly to ensure reasonable continuity between home and day care. Anti-racist measures, in matters such as books, dolls, music, pictures and home corner equipment, are also important in centres attended only by white children and adults, who otherwise learn racist attitudes (CRE 1996; Siraj-Blatchford 1996; Lane 1999). Emily and Pauline, aged three and four years, illustrate how crucially early years centres can affect how children feel about their personal and cultural identity (Brown 1998).

Emily, Pauline and Cinderella

Emily: Let's play Cinderella.

Pauline: That's a good idea. Can I be Cinderella?

Emily: No, you can't.

Pauline: Why not?

Emily: Because you're black.

Pauline: Why can't I be Cinderella because I'm black?

Emily: 'Cos Cinderella is white in my story book and on my video.

Anti-racist education aims to increase contact between people from different ethnic backgrounds by helping them to listen to one another respectfully, and to feel liked for who they are. An example of valuing different cultural backgrounds was given by staff in an Italian nursery where a newly-arrived Chinese baby was unhappy. Her carers learned to help her to become much happier by carrying her on their hips, as her parents did, by babbling and singing in 'Chinese' rather than Italian intonations, and by playing a tape of her father singing Chinese lullabies which the other children also enjoyed (Selleck and Griffin 1996). There are high numbers of young children in refugee and asylum-seeker families, who tend to live in temporary housing and to move on frequently, so that rapid flexible ways of welcoming these children and their parents are especially important (Rutter and Hyder 1998).

Anti-racist practice in the early years has been summarised in ways which include the following points (Brown 1989). Carers promote health and happiness by helping all young children to:

- feel relaxed, confident and secure;
- feel good about themselves and their families;
- feel that adults expect them to achieve and that these expectations are realistic;
- feel accepted and valued by other children and, in turn, to be able to reciprocate these feelings;
- be able to respond cooperatively to adults and to other children;
- trust and to feel at ease with adults;
- be exposed to as wide a range of suitable learning materials and situations as possible;
- be given encouragement and praise;
- be in an atmosphere in which they can feel a sense of belonging.

'When children's needs are met they blossom, when they are not, they suffer. Where there is an anti-racist approach, all children benefit. Where racism is allowed to flourish unchallenged, all children are disadvantaged' (Brown 1989).

Anti-racism can be encouraged or discouraged in many subtle ways. For example, staff may try to stop children from speaking their mother-tongue although research suggests that they learn English more quickly when they can use both languages. Or staff may try to insist that children who eat with their fingers at home use utensils at school (Lane 1999).

Children as young as four years make comments like: 'I don't like black people because they are bad on television.' Very young children are not immune to racism but can feel deeply hurt and excluded, bewildered or angry, unless they know they are valued. Black and Asian children can feel troubled about their identity in a 'white' world. All children can benefit from having black dolls and respectful books and pictures about black people, unless the children are left to use them in racist ways, and they need to talk about racial or cultural differences honestly.

Cruel treatment

'No child shall be subjected to torture or other cruel, inhuman or degrading treatment, or be deprived of his or her liberty unlawfully. Every child deprived of liberty shall be treated with humanity and respect for the inherent dignity of the human person' (37). State parties shall 'take all appropriate measures to promote physical and psychological recovery and social reintegration of a child victim' after neglect or abuse, cruel treatment or armed conflict (39).

One example of cruel treatment is the suffering children of prisoners often endure. Rates of women prisoners in Britain are rising rapidly for reasons such as debt or petty theft, which are associated with the increase in poverty among young and single parent families. Although babies can stay in prison, they have to leave at an age when close contact with their mother is still crucial, and families are not helped in their 'social reintegration'. In 1997, 125,000 children experienced one of their parents being sent to prison (Ramsden 1998). Some of them, aged four to fourteen years, were interviewed, and they spoke of their worry about being teased, losing friends, and being labelled themselves as bad. Children react differently. One six-year-old painted a face behind bars, suggesting perhaps that she wanted to talk to her teacher; another seemed to want to ignore the reality that her mother was in prison as much as she could; others are tearful or angry, showing that adults who hope to help them must first listen to children about how they would like to be supported.

These sections have touched on a few of the innumerable ways that provision and protection rights affect children's daily lives, as do also the participation rights in the next section.

(III) YOUNG CHILDREN AND PARTICIPATION

Provision and protection rights enjoy wide support, but participation rights are seen as more controversial. Yet, as this review shows, all three rights overlap.

Right to life and to optimal development

'Every child has the inherent right to life' (6) and to 'care as is necessary for his or her well-being' (3). State parties 'shall ensure to the maximum extent possible the survival and development of the child' (6).

These rights make all other rights possible.

Name, identity and family

'The child shall be registered immediately after birth and shall have the right to a name, the right to acquire a nationality and, as far as possible, the right to know and be cared for by his or her parents' (7). The child has the right 'to preserve his or her identity, including nationality, name and family relations' (8). And if the child is illegally deprived of these, there should be help 'with a view to speedily reestablishing his or her identity' (8). States should 'ensure recognition of the principles that both parents have common responsibilities for the upbringing and development of the child' (18). The child and parents should not be separated 'unless this is in the best interests of the child' (9).

The sense of identity which grows through continuing relationships is the basis for children to be seen, and to see themselves, as people to be consulted. Wide-ranging rights associated with the sense of personal identity include the right to know about your original parents' identity after adoption or assisted reproduction. (Snowden 1996). When babies are seen as respected persons from the start, as members of their family and their community, participation rights are a life-long process taking 'due account of the importance of the traditions and cultural values of each people for the protection and harmonious development of the child' (preamble). This includes attention to the culture of each child, such as in language, dress, music, art, food and religious ceremonies (30).

The right to a name involves other people in respecting the child's full name and not altering it, such as by shortening it or using a nickname against the child's wishes. Respect includes spelling and pronouncing the name properly, and not mixing up the personal and family name, as European people sometimes do with Asian names. The Muslim name Tahir, for example, begins with a sound between Th and D so that it takes some practice for European people to pronounce the name well. Mispronunciation can be especially offensive if it creates another word in the original language, and if the name has a religious meaning (Lane 1999).

Having a say

'State parties shall assure to the child who is capable of forming his or her own views the right to express those views freely in all matters affecting the child, the views of the child being given due weight in accordance with the age and maturity of the child' (12).

The key participation right is the right to express a view. At first, babies clearly express their views by making contented or unhappy noises. Modern methods of filming with electronic equipment show babies' expressive powers. Babies appear to be born with skilful abilities to communicate, such as in their 'micro-interactions', tiny head movements in time with the movements and sounds other people make when talking with them (Stern 1990).

Children are said to be egocentric. Everyone is self-centred to some extent, but the word does not fit much that babies do. They watch intently, react to other people's moods very sensitively, absorb and copy their behaviours such as facial expressions, and initiate interactions with them from their first days. Babies aged one month seem able to match shapes they have sucked with ones they look at (touch with vision); from four months they notice differences in numbers of objects; and at six months they seem able to perceive cause and effect and be surprised (staring hard, widening their eyes) at effects that appear to have no cause (Siegal 1997; Stern 1990). These abilities are not described here as 'mile stones' which babies should reach. Everyone varies and Einstein was said not to begin to talk until he was three-years-old. Instead, this book aims to show how babies are people with thoughts, feelings and rights, as other people close to them know, and to question academic and public opinions which dismiss babies' immense capacities.

Besides looking outwards and reacting to people and things around them well before used to be thought possible, babies express their views strongly and clearly through sounds and gestures, and in play when they make choices and show intense concentration and enjoyment. One study demonstrates this through a video showing a 21-day-old baby at play with an older baby for 20 minutes as they make sounds and touch each other (Goldschmeid and Selleck 1996). As infants start to use words, they make their views and wishes still more clearly known, unless they are strongly discouraged from doing so. The right to express a view and to be responded to begins to be honoured or withheld from birth and is soon expressed through sophisticated activities.

Henry, Harriet and Natalie

Henry (six months) sat watching Harriet (six years) patting her legs and clapping her hands and he patted his own legs and clapped his hands. As she rolled a ball to him he held out his hands ready to take the ball, held and sucked it, and then jerked his arms to push it away, as if trying to throw, and watched where the ball rolled. His rocking music box stopped playing music so he casually batted it to restart the music. Harriet looked at something behind Henry and he turned to follow her gaze. Then she pulled a caterpillar on a string towards him. Henry grasped the string and drew the toy towards himself. Harriet passed him a coloured box covered with shapes which make different sounds when pressed. Henry looked very pleased and banged the shapes, smiling at the sounds. Later, he grabbed his teddy, cuddled it and chewed its ear. He leaned forwards and sideways to reach other toys as if trying to work out how to crawl to them. When given a piece of apple he held it carefully and bit off a lump. Often placid and watchful, Henry became excited when his friend Natalie (five months) arrived. Natalie waved her arms up and down with pleasure, smiled and made happy noises at Henry. Natalie's mother sat her near to Henry and the babies reached eagerly towards each other.

Henry shows a few of the many ways in which babies 'form and express a view' (12), in responding differently to each object and event, showing his interest and pleasure and, perhaps most importantly, constantly creating and recreating his relationships with other people through copying them, playing, greeting, and sensitively responding in many other ways.

Later, as tape recordings of four-year-old girls show, young children hold rich, deeply thoughtful daily conversations (Tizard and Hughes 1984). Frequently they ask questions such as, 'Why do ships float?' and 'Does the queen always wear a crown?' Ways in which young children share in making decisions that affect them are reviewed in Chapter 8, as this chapter is mainly about the beginnings of respecting children's rights.

Body language

Hasid, aged four, who does not speak, was having difficulty at meal times. The speech therapist working with his helper at school suggested better seating positions and liquidising his food slightly more. That helped to improve his feeding skills and reduced the risk of choking. The therapist advised his helper to remember to go slowly, and give him time to respond, to wait for signs from him that he wanted more food. He has always enjoyed having his food, but he had just been in hospital having surgery, and was uncomfortable and still adjusting to coming back to school. The school staff thought: 'Maybe he's taken a few steps back after making a lot of progress. So maybe we have to go a few steps back with him in every area, in order to move on' (Cleves 1999).

Right to be heard during procedures

'...The child shall in particular be provided the opportunity to be heard in any judicial or administrative proceedings affecting the child, either directly, or through a representative or appropriate body...'(12).

Part of the right to express a view is the right to explain and to appeal in serious matters such as being excluded from school. Even some four-year-olds are among the thousands of children each year excluded from school (Children's Society 1998), with no right in English law to speak to the adults who decide to exclude them, or to appeal. The UN Committee on the Rights of the Child was disturbed about this omission (UN 1995). One researcher commented: 'Exclusion of infants shouldn't be an option' (Parsons 1996). As numbers of exclusions from similar schools vary so greatly, some excluding no children at all, it seems that this is a reflection of school policy rather than of children's behaviour. Centres in London and Bradford, for example, help to prevent exclusions by working with many three and four year olds who find it extra hard to settle into their schools. The next example shows how listening to children can helpfully expand well beyond formal disciplinary hearings into working with them on changing their distressed behaviour.

Disruptive and distressed behaviour

Janet (22 months) ran around frenetically at home and all around the whole nursery, making everyone anxious. Her key worker, Helen, listed the many things Janet could do, which helped the staff to feel more hopeful. Helen began by running with Janet in the garden, holding her hand. She wanted to slow Janet down and help her to gain more skill and control in movement, in close relationship to her adult. Helen would hold Janet in her arms until she relaxed and was able to enjoy the treasure basket, mouthing objects as if she were a much younger child. Later Janet began to put objects in and out of containers, while the nursery organiser discussed these approaches with Janet's mother. After a few days of intensive attention, Janet became more like an ordinary energetic child, and the staff found there were many ways of helping her to be more calm and attentive. The staff had decided not to wait for weeks until Janet saw a paediatrician before beginning their programme to help her. Even when a doctor had seen her, a medical diagnosis would still leave the staff to have to devise practical ways of helping Janet (Goldschmeid and Jackson 1994).

Janet illustrates how behaviour problems, even ones with serious medical names, can be greatly relieved (or increased) by ways the adults consult and learn from the child and adapt their minute-by-minute care.

Freedom of expression and information

'The child shall have the right: to freedom of expression [including] freedom to seek, receive and impart information and ideas of all kinds, regardless of frontiers, either orally, in writing or in print, in the form of art, or through any other media of the child's choice' (13).

Jacqueline

Jacqueline (17 months) sat with her legs stretched in front of her near a heap of ribbons and chains. She chose a red ribbon and laid it across her ankles, then laid a chain two inches higher parallel, then a yellow ribbon, repeatedly alternating a ribbon and a chain to just above her knees. She looked at them intently and smiled to herself (Goldschmeid and Jackson 1994).

In this playing, babies make choices, are independent and creative. They cannot do it 'wrong' or make mistakes. Jacqueline devised her own rules and purposes, and concentrated on creating. Babies can be deeply satisfied with colours, shapes and patterns and with rearranging them. The following examples about the treasure basket show babies' fascination with objects and with using things to express and deepen these relationships with other people.

The treasure basket is a low basket filled with ordinary objects for babies to select and handle. When only a few months old they can be propped up to play with it.

> Babies, though intent on handling their own chosen objects, are very clearly not only aware of each other, but are engaged much of the time in active interchanges. It is the availability of the objects that stimulates these exchanges, which sometimes develop into little tussles for possession. These interchanges with other babies are different from those which they have with adults...it is the other baby and the objects of common interest which hold their energy within the context of the attentive adult's presence... However, the interchange of intense looking, of glances, smiles, proverbial noises of great variety, touching each other and sharing objects, all spring directly from the experiences babies have with their close adults (Goldschmeid and Jackson 1994).

A ten-month-old boy sitting at his mother's feet played with the treasure basket. He tried to pick up a large pebble with one hand and then managed that with two. He lightly gnawed the roughish surface making a grating noise which made the watching adults shudder. Seeing this, the baby gnawed again while watching the adults who began to laugh. During the next 40 minutes, he gnawed again twice, watching the adults' amusement intently.

If children's instincts to explore have been strongly discouraged, it may take much gentle encouragement before they are confident to express themselves such as by reaching out to grasp objects.

For people to be able to have informed views, adequate information is essential. Children gather information in many ways, through their senses, by watching and copying others, by testing objects and people, as well as by being informed and taught by others (Selleck and Griffin 1996; Elfer and Selleck, in press). Babies develop trust (or mistrust) in their carers and willingness to cooperate with them (or not), through their experiences of being treated gently or roughly. They respond to reassuring explanations before they understand words, and they learn to talk by being spoken to for months beforehand, as if they can already talk. 'Information' includes physical contact and other body language, games, pointing and holding objects and pictures, feeding and playing, and many other means of supplementing or replacing words. Information surrounds babies in the constant examples they see of how other people interact, which they soon imitate.

From the second year, telling a story can help children to understand and cooperate with stressful experiences like having hospital treatment. It is as if the story format describing the treatment and how they will go home afterwards helps children to make sense of the ordeal. A story with toys and pictures can help children as young as three years to cope, for example, with major surgery (Alderson 1993). One way that children help one another to digest and come to terms with new information and experiences is through playing partly imaginative games together, such as about a new baby arriving or a daddy leaving. The QCA (1998) advises that by the end of Key Stage 4, 14-year-olds should be able to express and understand another person's point of view, and yet young children do this daily when, for example, they play in the home corner.

Extra information

Some children need extra information. For example, blind babies lie very still in order to hear intently when someone enters the room. If they are suddenly picked up, they become very distressed. Their parents are upset because they expect the baby to be pleased when they arrive. If the parents talk to the baby as they enter the room, the baby understands, enjoys their arrival, and wants to be picked up.

Freedom of expression may require extra aids such as Makaton signing for children who do not talk, or double bikes so that children of different physical abilities can ride around in pairs. Many ideas increase the scope for all children to express themselves more fully as shown at Save the Children's Equal Opportunity Centre in London (and Cleves 1999).

In a sense, information is power, helping the child to have security through some understanding and sense of control, instead of feeling suspended in helpless uncertainty, at the mercy of unknown powers. Children are then better able to see how to cooperate instead of making fearful protests. Like other rights, the child's right to information is qualified to prevent harm to the child and to others.

Freedom of thought, conscience and association

The child has the right to 'freedom of thought, conscience and religion' (14) and to 'association and peaceful assembly' (15), subject to all the conditions listed at the beginning of this chapter on rights.

These rights raise questions about respecting young children's sense of awe and wonder, and their understanding of right and wrong, and of making moral choices which are shown from the second year (Dunn 1995). Since writing 'from the second year' I have watched a nine-month-old boy absorbed for hours in watching a JCB, which he calls 'dig dig', with awe and wonder at its power. Again, these capacities cannot be linked to an age; new-born babies' intense feelings of pleasure or fear can also be seen as awe and wonder.

Respect involves reserving judgement about whether children are 'good or bad', trying to understand their behaviours from their point of view, and encouraging their loving respect for other people's thoughts and feelings. Freedom of religion, association and peaceful assembly are important rights for families to enjoy so that babies can live as members of free communities, enjoying public spaces and gatherings, including parties, religious meetings, weddings and funerals. As symbols of hope and renewal babies can bring profound meaning to these ceremonies. Moral awareness begins very early. When children are aware of the difference between hurting or fighting and of helping and sharing with other people, or when they argue about how should have the biggest biscuit, they are thinking about concepts of kindness and justice.

Learning freedom of conscience

Emma (14 months) usually did as she was asked, and as she became more mobile, dangerous things were lifted out of her reach. One day she touched a gas-fire tap in a house she was visiting. Her mother said: 'No, no, don't touch that, it will hurt you, please come over here, come on.' For the first time, Emma looked as if she realised that she could choose whether to cooperate with her mother or not. She paused, with a look of surprise, interest and perhaps of pleasure and alarm. Her mother felt this was a great moment in their relationship, when she had to choose whether to appeal to Emma's new capacity to make decisions, her conscience, or else firmly overrule her, by force if necessary. Emma touched the tap again as if to test her mother, who repeated her words very firmly and seriously. Emma looked as if she decided to believe her mother's tone and look of great concern for her welfare, and she moved away from the tap. These can be decisive moments when, in new ways, parents try pleading that can sound too weak, or force that is too strong, or else a kind of confident consulting, a direct appeal to the child's reason, sense and trust.

The main aspects of citizenship have been defined as social and moral responsibility, community involvement and political knowledge (QCA 1998), (politics involves how power and resources are shared out). Children learn about these through doing them, such as talking about how to share, take turns, or plan events they can enjoy together. Research with children about their rights found direct, practical and responsible understanding among all age groups in the survey of seven to seventeen-year-olds (Alderson 1999).

Children aged eight also knew when teachers avoided practical respect for human rights by trivialising or distancing them: 'It's so boring when they keep telling you that making the world a better place means picking up litter and not killing whales.' Incidentally, they showed their interest in rights, besides their ability to complete a 20-page questionnaire; the youngest group was most likely to say that they found the booklet interesting (88 per cent). They were sceptical when rhetoric about democracy did not fit the reality in their schools, and knew whether their school council was token or genuine. Eight-year-olds said: 'The council meetings aren't much good because we have to write the newsletter then, and we can't discuss things.' In another school, pupils this age kept notes and reported between their classes and the effective council meetings. Primary schools councils have helped to raise standards of behaviour in the school, reduce bullying and other problems, end the need for exclusions, train pupils in other schools and run a farm (QCA 1998).

Sharing responsibility

With a group of 20 children aged up to four years, the staff decided that the children could help themselves to fruit and water when they wanted to. At first, the children asked for permission until they learned they could help themselves. Some spilt the water but they helped to mop up the spills and learned to pour more carefully, as they became used to doing so. In being consulted in this practical way about what they actually preferred and could do, the children were able to behave more responsibly and the staff were free to do other things (Miller 1997).

Mass media

State parties shall 'encourage the mass media to disseminate information and material of social and cultural benefit to the child and in accordance with the spirit of the [Convention] ... especially [materials] aimed at the promotion of his or her social, spiritual and moral well-being and physical and mental health' (17).

Besides providing children with entertainment and information to enlarge their understanding, the media have a strong influence through promoting positive images of children, or unfairly negative images which, by frequently denigrating children, make it harder for adults to take them seriously. An article picked at random illustrates common themes, which journalists presumably find appeal to the public. Called 'Want a baby? Read this first', the article describes how a mother's 'romantic notions of family life' were destroyed by the strain of having a baby whose father has now left the home. The mother works part time as a model, is taking a degree course, cares for her baby, and 'has no time left for herself', as if somehow she is not herself while doing these things. The baby is implicitly blamed for increasing the strains which existed between her parents before she was born (Morris 1999). The media reflect and reinforce public attitudes and policies, such as to cut benefits to single mothers and exhort them to find paid work. Implicit in this policy is that any paid work, however menial, pointless or mechanical, is better than caring for children. Even when child-care workers are paid, they tend to be seen as having low social status. NNEB students, when asked to name 'masculine' work that compares with 'feminine' child care work, said 'rubbish collection' (Penn 1997b).

The media share in driving young children away from enjoying public places, partly through sensational stories about strangers and dangers, partly because adults fear being publicly blamed through the mass media if children they care for get into danger. Children and teenagers are the last groups still to be dismissed in adverse stereotypes, in ways which journalists would no longer risk applying to women, or black, or gay people.

Children's Express

The staff on the Children's Express work as reporters aged 8–13 who conduct penetrating interviews, and as editors aged 14–18. Most of them come 'from backgrounds which offer little op-portunity', and they publish reports in many newspapers and magazines. Recently, 27 of them monitored 400 stories in the national press to find that every article stereotyped children – as victims, cute, evil, exceptionally excelling, corrupted, as ac-cessories to adults or as 'brave little angels'. They held a con-ference in 1998 (Kids these days) to publicise their research (Neustatter 1998).

Inclusive communities

'A mentally or physically disabled child should enjoy a full and decent life, in conditions which ensure dignity, promote self-reliance, and facilitate the child's active participation in the community'. The event-ual aim for all services for disabled children should 'be conducive to the child's achieving the fullest possible social integration and individual development' (23). International understanding, skills and capabilities in the care of these children should be improved, according to the Convention.

Siobhan

Siobhan's mother June 'fought' to get her into mainstream nursery school, and felt criticised by teachers and other parents. 'They looked at me as if I was crazy... Somebody said to me: "I don't think you've accepted your daughter's disability," and I said: "Well I live with it, of course I've accepted it." So it was more harder for me to take Siobhan to mainstream than to special because I had people [adults] staring at me. But once they got to know me, all that was gone... As far as I was concerned, the *children* were accepting her. I think because she was in from the age of three, the children didn't have the hang-ups that the adults had, I think they found it easier and that made me more determined then to keep Siobhan at mainstream... Things that the teachers or even me as a parent would be frightened to attempt for Siobhan, such as climbing on the frames, getting on the swings, they saw a way round it. And she'd manage to get up the top of the slide and there would be people around saying "Oh God, no," but the children always saw a way round and got her down, where adults were frightened to master that part.'

Perhaps the confidence she gained during her early years through playing and taking risks helped Siobhan during the 'kind of horrible time' when she started at her secondary school to wait for months in the school entrance until lessons were rearranged and a lift installed for her to reach the classrooms. Now, she is happier about the teachers: 'I suppose they wasn't really sure how to approach me and what to say, kind of, if they said something would they hurt my feelings...talking down to you, would I understand. [Now] they talk to me more personal, suiting my age.'

June added: 'It would be nice to protect Siobhan, I mean I'd love it as [her] mum, but that's not what I wanted. I wanted Siobhan to face the world as it was going to be' (Alderson and Goodey 1998).

One reason for referring disabled and disturbed children to special schools is that 'other children will be cruel to them'. Yet there are many examples of young children helping disabled children to learn and play (Lewis 1994), to climb, explore and take reasonable risks. Disabled children are often outgoing, friendly and adventurous and they have much to offer to people in mainstream schools (Herbert and Moir 1996; Cleves 1999; Audit Commission 1992). It is sometimes said that young children do not notice difference or disability, but it seems that they are very aware of differences, and make allowances without judging others as better or worse, more or less able. Is also seems that often the children who are seen as difficult, or 'tougher' and 'harder', and the disabled children themselves, rather than the adults, lead in making their groups or classes more inclusive.

These are a few ways in which the comprehensive UN Convention on the Rights of the Child support young children's rights to be consulted. The UK Agenda for children reviews many further ways of doing so (Lansdown and Newell 1994). Children's rights are carefully qualified in the Convention to defend the interests of children, adults and society. As formal entitlements, rights protect children from having to rely on adults happening to be kind, but rights also support such kindness, they complement welfare measures, and they show how young children can actively contribute to their families and communities.

CHAPTER TWO

Young Children as People

IMAGES OF CHILDHOOD

People sometimes ask, 'Do you mean children should have adult rights?' This chapter looks at meanings of child, adult and human being, beginning with examples of varied childhoods, followed by theories of child development. Further examples of children's abilities lead on to considering their status as human beings.

Histories of childhood, and reports of research today across the world, show how greatly varied childhoods are (Aries 1962; Hardyment 1984; Hendrick 1997). Here is one historical example.

William Blake, England c.1800

'At seven years of age I was set to work in the silk mills, where I toiled from five o'clock in the morning till seven at night for the weekly sum of one shilling. This paid for my board and lodging, and rendered me independent of my father except for the clothes I wore.

There, a remarkable circumstance occurred to me. Afraid of being past my hour in the morning, and deceived by a clouded moon, I frequently rose in the night mistaking it for day. At one of these times, I found all was silent in the mill, and I knew that I was too early. As I stood leaning pensively on the parapet of the bridge, I heard the clattering of horses' feet; and, without turning my head, I asked what it was o'clock. No answer being given I turned to look, and I distinctly saw the appearance of a man, riding one horse and leading another, on the mill wheel. The clock then struck four, and the apparition vanished' (Rosen 1998).

The example shows the high demands made on working children's energy and time in the belief that this was normal. Today in Outer Mongolia, children start school at eight years. Before that, they work as herders and some spend all day wandering alone with their goats in temperatures of plus or minus 40 degrees (Penn 1998a). Again, this is seen as normal.

These examples tend to be compared with the lives of children in the UK today, as if we now know how to treat children properly because we understand what it really means to be a child. Yet the examples say far more than this. They show how our images of childhood are no more real than those examples are, except in the way our images construct and reflect the lives of children in our society, just as other images reflect other societies. Children's health and perhaps the happiness of most children have improved in the UK since the 1800s, but they have lost independence and status – William Blake thought it right to be independent at seven.

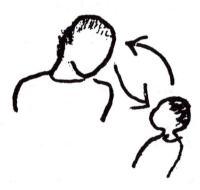

Figure 2.1 Adults and children construct and reconstruct one another, for example, as having very different levels of understanding or as sharing more equal insights

The images of childhood also show how adults and children continuously construct and reconstruct their beliefs about childhood in their daily talk and behaviour (Figure 2.1). Anne Solberg described how four-year-olds showed her that she was talking down to them and infantilising them during research interviews. With their help she established more equal relationships and she interviewed the children for up to an hour about 'what did you do yesterday?' (Solberg 1993).

After their first few weeks or months of life, children are not inevitably and in every way dependent, though many are treated in ways that stop them from becoming independent (CRO 1995b). The next three examples, about changes in the way young children use the streets during this century, illustrate this.

Albert Parr remembered that when he was aged four, in the 1900s in Stavanger, Norway, he enjoyed walking to the station alone for five or ten minutes, buying a ticket, watching the trains and riding over the long bridge to the harbour. He watched the boats, sometimes went into the fisheries museum, passed the park where the band played, or the shops or the fire station, explored the fish market, selected and haggled for the fish, bought them and returned home (Parr 1994).

Margaret and Elizabeth

In 1902, Elizabeth, aged three, had been in hospital for months. A message was sent to her mother at the other side of Derby to fetch Elizabeth. As her mother was at home in labour, she sent Margaret, aged five, with a push chair to collect her sister. Now in her nineties, Margaret remembers that the matron asked: 'Where is your mother?' and was annoyed when Margaret replied: 'In bed.' Margaret took Elizabeth who screamed all the way home. Both her mother and the matron assumed that Margaret was old enough to do this.

Kevin aged five and Alan aged seven, in 1998, were boisterous, rather tough-looking boys who lived in a small rural town. They walked to school with their mother, the school gate being about 90 seconds walk away within sight of their home. They lived in a busy side road lined with parked cars, and many drivers regularly exceeded the speed limit. One day, Alan was ill and their mother told Kevin to walk on his own to school while she watched from the front door. After a short way, he ran back crying and very frightened. Like many of his friends, he had never walked alone along the street before.

These examples raise questions about how adults' fear about risk and lack of confidence in children limit how adults can consult and trust children.

Another colouring of adults' views of children comes from adults' memories of their own happy or unhappy childhoods and, for example, their delight or envy when seeing happy children. William Blake, who appeared earlier in this chapter, aged seven years, as an adult wrote pairs of happy and sad poems about childhood including two nurses' songs (Blake 1958, pp.37 and 47). At sunset the nurses call the children home to bed and the children say they want to go on playing. The first nurse lets the children play until the light fades and

> The little ones leaped & shouted & laugh'd
>
> And all the hills echoed.

The second nurse her 'face green and pale' tells the children to come home saying,

> Your spring & your day are wasted in play,
>
> And your winter and night in disguise.

In another poem 'The echoing green'(pp.27–8), old people remembering their own childhoods laugh while the children play. Children's voices echo through the ages, respected or repressed by adults, heard clearly or misheard, heard with pleasure or pain, interest or irritation. Children's echoes are blurred by the echoes of the listening adults' own childhood memories and present values, and by resounding myths about young children's inabilities.

DEVELOPING CHILDREN

Public and academic discussions about children are dominated by notions of 'development', and of 'early experiences as the path to the whole person'. People still repeat theories of the developing mind as if these are factual, and as if children's minds develop like their bodies through one universal pattern of ascending growth marked out by 'mile stones' from zero to adult maturity. These views strongly influence public opinion, as well as all the professions which work with children or advise or comment on their care (Hart 1998, pp. 27–30). Developed since the 1900s, these theories have had positive effects on children's lives, but they have also misunderstood and dismissed young children's capacities, and so discouraged adults from trusting and consulting children.

For example, guidance right across North America (National Association of the Education of Young Children 1992) covers the topics of protecting and providing for children and being advocates for them, of basing work on knowledge of child development and other adult expertise, and of consulting all concerned with the child including families and colleagues. Yet it does not mention asking children or taking any account of their views.

A book about how to fit observations of children to 23 pages about mile stones of development sums up ten whole months in these words: 'Key features of 9–18 months. Growing independence can lead to rage when thwarted. Shows anxiety when left alone. Emotionally more stable but can be jealous of adults' attention to other children. Can be defiant – learns NO' (Sharman, Cross and Vennis 1995).

The text concentrates on children's unreasonableness and limitations which make trusting them impossible. Another book by many early-years specialists is far more positive, and gives fine examples of competent children, their helpfulness, and imaginative awareness of others (Early Childhood Education Forum 1998, pp. 22–3):

Max (30 months) is just out of nappies and is expertly washing up his bowl. Suddenly he feels urine running down his legs. He watches anxiously at first and then, when one of the staff smiles at him, he smiles. Unasked, a three and a half-year-old friend brings a small mop, and finishes off the washing up, while Max mops up the puddle.

Yet the book still discusses even children aged three to five years as if they do not yet fully exist with headings such as 'being and becoming'.

Children learn to belong and connect in their relationships as they explore the possibilities of life in groups...they use all manner of materials...they learn about the constraints and difficulties of joining in...they are learning about choices and boundaries...in all this children are being and becoming their unique selves...learning that they can make significant contributions to their social relationships...opening new doors and

windows on the world [as] they handle bricks and blocks...
(Early Childhood Education Forum 1998, pp.32–3).

In one way all this is true, but in three other ways it is false. First, children are not simply learning and practising, they are living and accomplishing. Second, these words do not apply only to this age group, they describe Henry (aged six months in the previous chapter), and adults of any age who learn and relearn in new situations. Third, the words imply that adults are somehow 'developed', complete, so that in conflicts between them and children, adults are dangerously encouraged to assume that they are right and the child is wrong. This encourages and endorses adult control and coercion, instead of humility and reasoned negotiation.

It is as if the new understanding of babies' humanity can still only partly be seen through the fog of older theories about the slowly developing child, formulated by Piaget and others from the 1920s (Piaget 1924). New evidence of babies' abilities cannot fully be appreciated because of continuing attempts to distort and squeeze experience into stages (Burman 1994). Theories of stages of child development have been called 'misleading and oppressive' (Mayall 1994b, p.3) because of the ways they are used to misjudge, control and denigrate children. This is shown in quite sympathetic guidance for parents, as illustrated in the next two examples.

One BBC programme played a tape of Heather aged two, sister of a new baby, saying 'no' many times. The presenter commented that Heather could be in the Guinness book of records, and emphasised the patience needed by mothers and the huge demands made by children. Yet this ignored the context, and the transcript in the book accompanying the programme (Purves and Selleck 1999, p.44) omitted the end of the conversation – which sounded partly like a game. Heather said 'no' to all the comforting and 'babying' offers from her mother, of raisins, a cuddle, and so on. She finally said 'yes' when her mother suggested a shared, more responsible activity 'shall we go to the shops?'. Perhaps Heather was partly saying she did not, just then and contrary to the programme's implications, want to be infantilised. Asking children to help in an 'adult' way, respecting their worth and dignity, is often a way to resolve disagreements with them.

The second example in a best-selling baby book also blames problems on to age-stage and not other factors: 'Temper tantrums. Her ambitions far outreach her abilities. The resulting combination of stub-bornness and frustration can be explosive, resulting in the classic temper tantrum' (Stoppard 1998). Yet like anyone, two-year-olds can do lots of things well if other people give them time and do not insist on unrealistic standards. Frustration often arises when fraught rushed adults impose demands and restrictions. But this is not mentioned, and neither are the societies where the 'classic temper tantrum' is not a regular feature.

Notions of inexorable stages of life, such as the 'terrible twos', are like racism except that, instead of blaming skin colour, another part of biology, age, is blamed without reference to context. These theories with their 'rotten' unscientific foundations in Darwinian philosophy have been called the 'biologising of childhood' (Morss 1990; and see Siegal 1997) which diminishes understanding of the humanity of children. It takes at least two people to have a row, which is usually a power struggle. Adults have the most power but 'terrible twos' and other slogans not only absolve adults from questioning their own possible use or abuse of power, the slogans also endorse firmer or harsher adult control, by suggesting that volatile young children are out of control. Young children need responsible adult care and this involves treating them as reasonable people.

Some social psychologists criticise the emphasis in child develop-ment theories on 'normal, natural and needs' and advocate moving from a judging and measuring approach towards 'context, culture and competencies' instead (Woodhead 1998). By 'normal' they mean that a descriptive average among an examined group of Anglo-American children, such as their height at a certain age, is turned into a pre-scriptive 'normal' height, which all children are supposed to be near. Being 'too' short is taken as 'subnormal' and a problem which might need to be treated. Ideas of what is normal are reinforced by assump-tions about what is natural and correct, although average heights for the 17 per cent of children in richer countries have been rising throughout this century, and differ from average heights for all the children in the world. Abilities are similarly measured for 'normality' without taking much account of how much children's abilities vary depending on how and where they are tested, how much help with the task or previous experience they have, and many other factors. Thus, ability is turned into a static thing, instead of being seen as widely-varying responses depending on the context and relationships concerned. Norms set by professionals become the basis on which professionals prescribe and sometimes impose 'needs' (Woodhead 1997) which are defined in the belief that children who are different 'need' adults to restore them to normality, or to compensate for the tested differences, as in social educational needs. Sometimes such help is very useful but it is being defined and given in increasingly rigid ways as young children are subjected to a growing battery of tests by education and health specialists.

Given the great range of childhoods experienced across the world, psychologists who propose a universal pattern of normal child development have been compared with goldfish imagining that their bowl is the whole world (Woodhead 1999). The alternative approach is to see how children's abilities vary according to the expectations and experiences of children and adults in each culture. People have a range of abilities, like warmly welcoming friends or learning a language, which rise and fall and are learned or forgotten according to many factors including experience, context and personality. Instead of assuming that before certain ages it is useless to consult children on some matters, it is possible to see that children might partly-understand enough to be consulted on these matters or on some aspects of them, or they might understand if asked in different ways. Examples of very able young children may be seen as interesting exceptions that prove the rule, or which slightly stretch age or stage development levels, like new wine in old wine skins. Alternatively, this evidence is taken to disprove age-stage theories, and to show the need for new theories which appreciate the capacities and potential in young children, and new methods for nurturing these capacities. If this is to happen, older theories which block new approaches have to be rethought. The next section gives one example.

SPATIAL, MORAL AND REAL AWARENESS

A well-known example from child development is used here to show why young children's thinking and morality are so often under-estimated. Piaget set out to prove scientifically Freud's theory that children are self-centred or egocentric (Bradley 1989). He showed a model of three mountains with a doll to Swiss children, and asked them to identify the doll's viewpoint, such as by choosing one picture from ten which fitted the view which they would see if they stood in the doll's position (Piaget and Inhelder 1956). Few children under eight or nine years could pass this test, and children aged up to seven tended to pick the picture which fitted their own viewpoint, not the doll's.

Piaget concluded that children cannot fully understand that other people have a different viewpoint from their own, until they are aged seven or older (Piaget 1932). He thought that young children cannot realise that their own view is one among others, and they cannot separate themselves properly from other people, so they have a false idea of reality and identity, and their reports are unreliable. Piaget's findings were repeated in tests around the world, and were used to validate common beliefs in children's cognitive and moral immaturity, so undermining adults' sense of obligation to respect children's views.

Scottish researchers rephrased the question and asked children how a naughty boy could hide from one and then two policemen, and they even added two or three more mountains/partitions to the original three mountains, and a third policeman. They found that children as young as three years could solve these tests. They concluded that the children's seeming inability lay in the original way they were questioned, and not in the children's limitations (Donaldson 1978). This later research about young children's higher abilities is crucial to any discussion about consulting children. Yet it is still much less quoted than Piaget's older work and the myths about young children's incompetence which that work supports. So, older beliefs about young children's ignorance, inexperience, unawareness, unrealistic and self-centred thinking continue to dominate professional and public beliefs about childhood (Stainton-Rogers and Stainton-Rogers 1992). They still convince many adults that they must protect and control children, without needing to consult them. Children's rights to respect for their worth and dignity cannot be realised while the old theories still dominate public and professional thinking.

ABLE YOUNG CHILDREN

Much other research supports the value of consulting children, and seeing how much they can achieve with a little help, called scaffolding because children build on hints and cues from helpers, and vivid direct discussions on their own terms, the use of human interest stories, and avoiding abstractions and impersonal tests that may confuse or intimidate them (Bruner 1966, 1980; Levine 1993).

Children can solve harder puzzles by working together in groups rather than by working on their own (Doise and Myng 1981). Summaries of numerous research studies show that by the age of five, children have very clear understanding of self and others, language and space, music and art, morality, physics and technology, much of which they will rely on for their life time (Gardner 1993). For example, physics graduates answer questions about trajectory correctly when these are asked through conventional university physics questions. Yet when they are asked questions about physics in unexpected ways, the graduates fall back on their basic, life-time knowledge – that of a five-year-old child.

Children are perhaps more likely to be seen as full people, and consulted as equal workers in countries when many children work and there are no laws to restrict their involvement. The next two examples show how fully young children can contribute.

Water in the village

In Uganda, many children are the first generation to attend school and they become health educators for the community. The 600 children at the primary school became concerned that animals used the village pond which was the main water supply. They spoke with the village leader who called a village meeting where the children presented poems and dramas about the value of clean water. As a result, children and adults worked together on cleaning the well pond and building a fence to keep out the animals, then celebrated with food and music (International Save the Children Alliance 1995, p. 236).

These disadvantaged, sometimes illiterate children showed a little of the great untapped capacities which ordinary children have, but which are often shown during adversity. When children live sheltered lives, in some ways fortunately, they have less opportunity to show their strengths, and then they are often assumed to lack them.

The restaurant

During their monthly meetings, New Delhi street-boys realised that they spent 75 per cent of their money on food. Twelve boys aged seven to seventeen took an intensive ten-day course on cooking, nutrition, cleanliness, looking after customers and book-keeping, and had help with renting a space for a restaurant. They took half-pay at first, saying: 'You can't expect to be an overnight success in this business, one has to bear losses for a while…and try very hard.' They gave free food to some street children, learned Chinese cooking to expand the menu, and planned to raise money to buy a van to take food to an area where there are many street children, financed by selling snacks in public places. They learned from their difficulties, and by applying knowledge and testing new ways of solving problems, by gathering ideas from the surrounding social conditions and by planning, implementing and testing responses from the young customers (Save the Children Alliance 1995, p. 237).

DRAWING ON CHILDREN'S MANY ABILITIES

In England, the national curriculum provides for broad ways of consulting children in appealing to their many interests and respecting their abilities. Five-year-olds can show how they combine understanding of abstract concepts with practical tasks, from making an electrical circuit to explaining forces such as balance, friction and gravity, from learning about religious faiths to developing awareness of time and maps. Yet to fulfil so many tasks in crowded classrooms involves limiting the time children have to talk and listen to one another and to the adults. There is less time for choices and negotiation. In the interests of the whole group, children often have to wait a long time for their turn, or interrupt activities they are immersed in when everyone has to move on to another activity.

Reading and writing are vital skills, but they hold back young children's thinking. At first, literacy is like Japanese to English children, another language. Talking is far quicker and easier, closer to children's speed and level of thinking than reading or writing are. People need to talk about their plans, activities, perceptions, interpretations, mistakes and speculations. Between what someone clearly knows, and clearly does not know, at the proximal zone of learning where ideas are beginning to be understood, it is helpful to put these into words and test them in discussion. When children are constantly stopped from discussing and expected to write, and then to copy out again, their learning becomes slower and more superficial (Nutbrown 1996b; McNamara and Moreton 1993, 1995, 1997), and the way children are able to act as a valuable resource to one another is lost.

Babies are very good at pacing themselves, working with deep concentration as long as they feel enthusiastic, and then changing to another activity, and returning to continue with the first one later. They organise their learning, such as by babbling and trying out sounds, repeating tasks over and over again, and picking up vast amounts of knowledge. This self-organisation is respected in many early years centres, but in schools it does not fit the prescribed national model. For example, the termly report for five-year-old Nicola, who reads to herself for hours for pleasure at home, criticised her for starting with great enthusiasm but then 'running out of steam', a tellingly-mechanical image. At first, she said fervently: 'I love school', but after a few weeks she said sadly: 'You do lots of hard work and you go and ask Miss Mallam if you've done enough, and she says, "Go back and do some more".' How much harder do children who find learning less easy and enjoyable find this approach? The national literacy hour involves children from four years of age – an hour is a very long time to anyone who feels forced to do something they do not enjoy.

Some schools manage to combine the varied activities within the literacy hour with self-directed learning, in which children plan their day and their chosen order of activities using diaries which they fill in each morning. The children work in large groups with teams of teachers and support staff who can arrange detailed preparation and flexible personal and group support to children throughout the day (Cleves 1999). Up to age eleven, the children's self-directed learning follows patterns taken for granted in many early years settings.

For some Italians teachers: 'Our image is of the child rich in potential, strong, powerful, competent and, most of all, connected to adults and other children…co-constructors of their knowledge and identity through relationships' (Edwards, Gandini and Forman 1998). These children know that other young children in their centre can create complicated projects, and they are excited and also highly-organised during long and difficult tasks. When children's knowledge and motivation are respected, with teachers standing back while children question and answer one another and make plans, then children's abilities can be seen more clearly (see also Griffiths 1998).

The dinosaur project

Italian five and six-years-olds spent four months on a dinosaur project, consulting books, drawing, talking and writing about them. In small groups and with many discussions, they built four-foot-high models, the girls used Styrofoam and the boys, because they chose wire and metal, needed more help from adults. The staff 'consulted' children by talking with them and also keeping detailed records of the children's talk which the staff then read and reread and discussed.

This rereading of the children's concerns led the staff to challenge the six most active children to draw a life-size dinosaur and find a way to hang it so that it would stand on its feet. The children slowly worked out how to enlarge small drawings to scale, they marked out a rectangle 27 by 9 metres on the sports field – someone thought of using toilet paper when they ran out of rods. The girls had decided to use horizontal lines and the boys used vertical lines in their small drawings, so later they used both sets of drawings to map out the larger outline. Then they found they could no longer use the sports ground and they had to design a smaller dinosaur, 13 by 6 metres, in the courtyard.

Most five-year-olds in the pre-school shared in painting the plastic sheeting *diplodocus*. The six children presented an animated report to the school of all their drawings, and all the stages of creating the dinosaur, and the many problems they had resolved together. The staff arranged pulleys along the sports-field fence and during a festival for the families the dinosaur was hoisted up. The children asked the mayor to find a permanent display place for the dinosaur which he agreed to do (Rankin 1998).

The staff in these Italian centres consult the children continuously, beginning when babies arrive and staff observe them closely, learn from their eating and sleeping patterns, and talk frequently with their parents. With babies with 'special rights' (who have extra difficulties) the process may go on for weeks or months while they gradually settle in and the staff get to know the baby's 'gifts and contributions' to the centre (C. Smith 1998, pp.199–214).

Figure 2.2 The child and adult taking and giving.

GIVING AND TAKING

A standard view of children is one of taking: absorbing their parents' time and energy, being expensive dependents, needing many education, health and other professionals to care for them. This view sees the child taking and the adult giving. Yet children bring love and joy into families, they share in household work, thousands of children, a few as young as three years, are the primary carers for a sick or disabled relative in the UK (Becker and Aldridge 1995). In most countries (the majority world of poorer countries where 83 per cent of people live) young children have adult-like tasks and responsibilities; they challenge the richer minority world's assumptions that children can only receive goods and services, and do not also contribute. Millions of young children share in field, street and house work and care for babies. Many are grossly exploited, but many prefer to work, at least part-time (Johnson, Hill and Ivan-Smith 1995; White 1996).

To involve children in daily tasks can be a practical way of consulting them and drawing on their skills, knowledge and ideas, as well as increasing these skills so that children have still more to offer. Young children who are seen as people are more likely to be consulted and relied on by adults.

An example of research with some of the poorest children in the world, Bangladeshi street children, shows how people who have no formal education and the least rights can value rights to respect and dignity very highly (Khan 1997). Five girls and six boys aged between ten to fifteen years were the researchers, and each morning they interviewed one or two people aged between seven to fifteen years, 51 in all, who had been on the streets for years. In the afternoons, they dictated all they could remember to adults who wrote the notes and the report. The young researchers talked though every stage and method of the research and every line of the reports. They copied an earlier project from the UK (West 1995). Gradually the researchers identified eleven priorities. Contrary to experts' views that these children most want and need health, education and care programmes, only two priorities refer to these: dislike of dirty rotten food, and wanting vocational education but not full-time schooling. All the other points were about problems caused by adults: torture, injustice, exploitation, cheating, name-calling, never using the child's own name, forcing the children to do unpleasant and 'bad' work, lack of an adult guardian who is essential for getting a good job and for tackling unjust police and bureaucracies. The children questioned 'why they cannot get a decent life, they should have equal rights'. The points are about keeping dignity and some independence. They illustrate how children's views cannot simply be guessed and assumed by adults, and that in a world controlled by adults, real help and support for children involves working closely with them, giving and taking.

This chapter began with the question, should children have adult rights? In the UK, children and teenagers are dependent, financially, legally, and in many other ways, and cannot have all the same rights that adults have. However, apart from adults' rights to work, to vote and to found a family, young children surely share many of the same inalienable human rights which adults enjoy. 'Adult' tends to mean competent, informed, wise, altruistic and reliable, and 'child' to mean incompetent, ignorant, foolish, selfish and unreliable. Examples like the ones in this chapter, showing how all these qualities are shared at all ages, challenge assumed sharp differences between child and adult, and by showing their shared humanity, the examples strengthen the case for equal respect for the worth and dignity and rights of all human beings.

CHAPTER THREE

Beliefs and Feelings About Consulting Young Children

Only 200 years ago in Britain, the human story looked very different. After a short infancy, many people joined the working adult population for the rest of their (short) lives. Society depended on this large working force. Today, the story is decades longer and has many chapters which are assumed to be biological, factual, inevitable: babyhood, infancy, the 'latent' period, adolescence sometimes stretching into the mid-20s, adulthood, retirement, being elderly, old age, frail old age. All the stages except adulthood are also seen as partly dependent. Yet this dependency is not integral to young and old people. They are not incapable of contributing efficiently. It is imposed by social structures such as efforts to reduce the labour market of employable people.

As structures and routines have changed, so too have attitudes and it is now commonly believed that children cannot contribute. This chapter considers some of these entrenched but fairly new ideas. Children today benefit from better provision and protection. Yet protection can easily expand into coercion and over-rigid control. It can set self-fulfilling low expectations, or increase contagious fear in adults and children about children's supposed inadequacies. Paradoxically, by denying children the chance to become street-wise, over-protection can make children more vulnerable to dangers, and less able to cope with them.

All beliefs and patterns of thinking have been compared with plumbing, in the following ways (Midgley 1996). They tend to be invisible and ignored until something goes obviously wrong, such as leaks or blockages. Then people realise how vitally their lives are affected by the hidden pipes (or beliefs), and see that the most practical thing to do is to sort out the (mental) plumbing. Before assuming that children can or should be consulted, it is vital to examine the beliefs which encourage adults to consult children or stop them from doing so.

Some common beliefs are listed here, so that readers can identify where they stand. Adults who work in pairs or groups could discuss their own positions, in order to reach some broad agreement. If adult colleagues disagree, efforts to consult children and act on what they say are likely not only to fail but also to be seen as proof that it is not worth trying to listen to children. The following lists could be used for group discussions, in which further beliefs could be added and debated. The beliefs are set out under three headings: the principles involved, the benefits or harms which follow consulting children, and how children can learn though being or not being consulted.

WHY SHOULD YOUNG CHILDREN BE CONSULTED IN MATTERS WHICH AFFECT THEM?

1A In principle, it is the right thing to do.

- Children, like adults, have the right to be consulted and to express their views (UN 1989). In some public services, there is a legal duty to consult them (Children Act, Department of Health 1989).

- Formal consultation methods, like circle times, planning groups, or school councils, show the adults' good faith and concern for principles of justice and respect.

- To consult children respects them, and thereby sets examples which help them to respect themselves and other people, as part of the duty of care which adults and children have towards others.

- From their second year, children have clear ideas about being fair and being kind to other people (Dunn 1993, 1995). These ideas can be nurtured early on, partly by involving children in semi-formal discussions about making plans or sorting out problems in the groups they belong to.

- Talking and listening help children and adults to see which plans, problems and values they share, and where they differ, or need to work towards agreement. Through doing so, individuals can see the justice of respecting one another's rights, and sometimes setting other people's wishes before their own.

- Part of responsible adult care is to be willing to explain to children, to be accountable to them, to set the example of negotiating through disagreements, and to expect children to do so too, instead of resorting to pressure or force.

1B There are benefits in consulting young children.

- Adults can give more effective care when they use information from children. Encouraging children to share in solving problems can channel their ideas and energy, and their unique viewpoints, into finding better solutions. As one child said on being consulted: 'It would be better to have lots of ideas rather than one' (Mepani and Emerson 1998).

- As examples from some day nurseries and children's homes show, groups of children have continued to be abused when no adults were willing to listen to them.

- Talking together while making decisions can help to prevent misunderstandings or disagreements, and children becoming anxious, or resisting what might 'be done to them'.

- Children who feel respected are likely to respect others and to follow positive examples set by adults and other children. Habits of consulting increase mutual trust, can decrease rivalry, rows, violence and stress, and provide effective ways for groups to cope with problems that arise.

- People are more committed to decisions which they have proposed and agreed, and they will want to make them work well. Otherwise, adults risk working against children, not with them.

- Sharing responsibility for making informed decisions, like how to spend an equipment budget, helps children to know more about the value and the limits of funds and resources. By having to think realistically about ways of working within constraints or disagreements, and choosing what to have and what to do without, they are less likely to blame adults or to expect too much from them.

- Knowing that they can choose sometimes can help people to accept the times when they cannot do so.

1C It is educational to consult children.

Besides contributing now, children will also contribute and gain in other ways.

- People learn through talking, putting new ideas into words and checking their own and each other's understanding (McNamara and Moreton 1997).

- When they are consulted, children can learn how to work well in groups, to listen, take turns, explain their views clearly and persuasively, share decision-making and responsibility, and they become skilled and confident. Choosing the rules for their group, for example, can teach children to make decisions in a fair and accountable way. Learning to think adventurously involves learning from making mistakes, with protective adult support.

- Part of education is to learn to think creatively, critically and independently, and to know how to question and disagree politely. The best way to learn these skills is through practice.

- Consulting children helps them to be and become responsible members of their family, peer groups and local community, and to be citizens in their local and national democracy.

Why should young children not be consulted in matters which affect them?

These are some of the counter arguments.

2A In principle, it is the wrong thing to do.

- Children have the right to be protected by adults and to rely on them; it is wrong to encourage them to question adults' views. A duty to consult children is not sensible, unless it involves simply listening to them with no need to take account of what they say. The child's best interests are paramount and only adults understand these.

- It is hard enough to consult adults and to ensure reports of their views are fair and representative. How can this be done with young children, whose views are unreliable?

- School councils often do not work well. Even with adults, school governors' meetings are often undemocratic. Certainly with the youngest children, this pretence of democracy is irrelevant to them and betrays true adult responsibility, justice and respect.

- To consult young children is to confuse and worry them, and the duty of care means just that, adults caring for children by not passing responsibility on to them, but letting them enjoy some years of carefree innocence.

- Young children do not yet have clear sensible views to express. Research shows that children cannot really understand morality until they are at least seven or eleven, so their views cannot count.

- If children and adults disagree, children must realise that adults know best and have to set limits and be the judges. Parents are the experts in their child, and other adults who work with children also have expertise through their wider training and experience. Some parents with only one or two children might be able to consult them, but many parents would not want to, and it is unfair to them if professionals teach children to expect to be consulted. Even if parents can discuss things with their one or two children, adults working with larger groups do not have time.

- Responsible staff insist that children keep to the standards expected by the average parent, and they are accountable to parents, tax payers and to their colleagues, not to children.

2B There are potential harms in consulting young children.

- Letting children imagine they can tell adults what to do, or letting them think they can get away with something once, only leads to trouble for everyone and to lower standards of control, safety and obedience. It wastes time and effort in pointless arguments.

- Pretending to consult children risks raising false expectations, children will then be disappointed, leading to loss of adult authority, and to rows and stress. Maybe a few insistent children will be given privileges, which is unfair.

- A few articulate children might have useful ideas, but it is favouritism to encourage them. Other quiet children might want something different. A trained professional such as a teacher knows what all the children need, and trying to consult them formally is an admission of failure. Children must learn to trust adults' leadership, and not to follow other children's ideas.

- Children live in a fantasy world of childhood, we should not spoil it by trying to explain budgets, which they will not understand anyway. They need to feel that adults have total control – even if we do not. Children cannot make informed decisions because this involves thinking about more aspects of a question, and more viewpoints than they can manage.

2C It is an abuse of education to consult young children.

- They are too self-centred to be able to work well enough in groups to share decision-making and responsibility, and they will be upset when they fail.
- Before anyone can think independently, they need far more knowledge than young children have; the skills they need now are to believe and remember what they are taught.
- Children will become responsible adults if they are set firm examples of responsible adult control.

DEEPER FEELINGS

Each side, for and against, raises important discussion questions, about why and whether it is wise or kind to consult young children. But deeper feelings underlie these beliefs. Changes in set routines, such as when adults decide to set up a method of consulting children, involve several levels.

behaviour	listening to children or deciding not to
knowledge	gathering, sharing and agreeing on information about consulting, and about children
beliefs	the kinds of comments listed above which tend to be stated openly
feelings	deeply held feelings which may not be consciously held.
	The more unaware people are about their feelings, the more strongly they may be influenced by them.

The example in the Introduction of the teacher's anxiety about a paper clip illustrates how one approach to such anxiety would be to talk about how serious the risk really might be, and whether it could be worth taking in order to promote mature responsibility among the pupils. Yet this would divert attention from the real barriers, which are the feelings that underlie all the pros and cons about consulting children just listed. The feelings can be summarised in these ways.

People in favour of consulting young children tend to feel:

- trust and optimism in young children's ability to think independently and creatively;
- respectful faith in children's unique and important knowledge, and their sense of responsibility and care towards other people;
- enjoyment and excitement in working cooperatively and adventurously with children in quite complex ways;
- enthusiasm in encouraging children to be self-reliant and interdependent;
- confidence that, though it is time-consuming, consulting children and sharing plans with them are vital and rewarding parts of caring for them.

People not in favour of consulting young children tend to feel:

- confidence in adults' superior knowledge and good sense;
- conviction that children are very unlike adults and need extremely careful protection and care;
- mistrust and a sense that young children cannot understand much, or give reliable accounts, or think sensibly;
- deep concern about children's vulnerability;
- anxiety that children are volatile, self-centred, and a potential danger to themselves and others;
- heavy responsibility and concern that the caring adults will be blamed unless they control children firmly and safely;
- worry that it is cruel and wrong to let children take on risks or responsibilities;
- scepticism and doubt about consulting children, feeling that it will not work, wastes time, and creates problems which could upset children.

People tend to have mixed feelings, and do not fall simply into either group. Yet the way they balance their feelings affects how they combine appropriate caution with willingness to trust young children. A study of hospital nurses found that nurses on every level of seniority tended to feel anxious mistrust towards nurses more junior than themselves, seeing them as irresponsible. Yet each nurse also felt angry about being wrongly mistrusted by all the nurses senior to herself (Menzies Lyth 1988). This pattern is common in groups, especially when there are very clear differences in age, experience and responsibility, as in early years settings. Plans to consult children touch on powerful feelings about risk and anxiety which need to be discussed if they are not to be like blocked pipes.

CHAPTER FOUR

Methods of Involving Young Children

Whereas Chapter 3 was concerned with thoughts and feelings, this chapter is about methods. It also looks at barriers to closer communication, and especially consulting, between adults and children, and how the barriers might be overcome. A main way of involving children is by consulting them. Yet 'consulting' tends to mean that the people who do the consulting have the upper hand. They decide what questions to ask, and what they wish to do with the answers. For example, if teachers, play specialists or nurses consult the people who use their services, they may leave out questions which the users would like to raise. The answers may not reflect people's real concerns, and might be used selectively and misleadingly. Children have even less say in services provided for them when only parents are consulted.

'Consulting' can also mean that the person consulted has the most knowledge and authority to select the correct questions and answers, and decide on the best action: a consultant surgeon, for instance. Can young children be respected as consultants in this sense? Either meaning of consulting suggests an imbalance. In one the consulter has the main control, in the other the consultant has. With young children, adults always have more control and responsibility, but can they partly share these with children? Can children suggest and help to make improvements in their care, ranging from general policies to small daily details, in some kind of partnership with the caring adults? 'Consulting' means 'to sit with' (Skeat 1983), which implies some equality, talking on the same level and sharing time together.

Consulting is easier between small groups when there are flexible options so that children's views can be respected through positive action. On a larger scale, there are no established ways to consult adults properly, let alone children. The only regular national polls, elections, ask for one cross against numerous known and unknown policies, between a few, little known candidates. No choice is offered on matters on which all the parties agree, and the voting rate may be low. Phone-ins, focus groups, and official public consultations publicise a wide range of views, but they neither indicate how representative the responses are, nor how to arbitrate fairly between conflicting interest groups. Like the newspapers they can undemocratically support an articulate minority in ways that further exclude and silence other groups, including children. On a small and large scale, consulters have to guard against tokenism, poorly-designed methods and questions, and misinterpretation of replies. Opinion polls, which do tackle these problems, still only contact relatively small numbers of people, and elections show how unreliable their reports can be. So the difficulties of consulting children have to be seen as largely arising from the inadequacies of consulting processes, and not of children. The next section reviews some main barriers and ways of tackling them.

PRACTICAL BARRIERS TO CONSULTING CHILDREN
Lack of time

It can be quicker to consult parents and other adults. In large groups of children, one way to increase talking time is to help the children become skilled at talking and working out their ideas in small groups, and the staff can go round listening to the groups in turn. Children tend to balk at abrupt questioning from strangers, such as nurses when they arrive in hospital. A few moments spent discussing their hobbies or pets first can help them to open up and be far more responsive. Yet busy professionals question whether this is the best way to use their own time. Adults learn subtle ways of silencing children, and many staff worry that they will be criticised for delays if they talk to children. These avoiding tactics can develop into habit and example among experienced practitioners. Those who make time to talk say that in the longer term this saves time when children are able to understand, for example, how to sort out maths or literacy problems, or to cooperate with medical treatment.

Lack of confidence

This tends to be accompanied with anxiety about making mistakes and looking foolish. Anything worth doing can be risky and involves making mistakes while gaining new skills. Research interviews with children and parents suggest that they are more interested in the goodwill of professionals who work with them, their sincere manner and intentions, than in slick communication skills.

Lack of skill in talking with children

This can be a restriction, though many people may be more adequate than they feel, and confidence grows with practice. All adults have been children and have talked with their peers, so this is partly a matter of remembering former skills. Some adults find that the best teachers are children themselves. The idea that talking to children is so different and complicated that it requires special courses is unhelpful, since it requires the same skills as talking to anyone else of any age. Helpful ways to approach any person include:

- to sit at about the same eye level;
- adapt the volume, tone and pace of talking to suit the other person;
- use a simple or more complex vocabulary as appropriate;
- word and rephrase questions clearly;
- wait attentively for answers;
- respect what is said and try to pick up and continue themes the person introduces;
- respond to funny or serious moods;

and

- try not to interrupt or dismiss what is said (see for example, Wipfler 1990; Hurley 1998; Ward 1997; Morris 1998).

Language can be a barrier

This occurs when the children or adults use pet words, colloquialisms, jargon and any terms which are unfamiliar to the other person. This occurs at all ages, though young children tend to use more personal words. Parents can be helpful two-way interpreters. When English is an additional language for the child and an interpreter is needed, it is important to have someone who respects young children and is skilful at talking with them together with their parents. Extra time, patience and perseverance may be required. Words are often supplemented by body language, sighs, cries, and laughter. Drawings, acting, games, toys and visual aids can also enrich mutual understanding.

Family dynamics

To address children directly may challenge family dynamics. Although many parents gently encourage their child to take a growing share in the conversation, or are pleased about their child's independence, some parents wish to dominate the interaction. The mid-years alliance, the assumption that adults speak to adults and that children (or elderly people) listen, is powerful. It can require tact and confidence to resist deferring to the parents without offending them when trying to consult the child.

Fear of losing control

This drives some adults to avoid consulting children when they want to get on with their work quickly, in case the child might refuse, dawdle, start an argument or resort to other time-wasting tactics. In schools, for example, some staff worry that if they are too friendly, children will try to play power games – and win. To cope with this, many professionals skilfully combine friendly respect with firm confidence.

Anxiety about children's distress

If children have serious difficulties adults' anxiety can be a major constraint. Adults worry about: which topics the child might raise, and about unanswerable questions, pleas for help which cannot be prom-ised, long personal accounts which hardly seem relevant, and cries of anguish and despair. Such difficulties span the age groups, and there are books and teaching videos on how to respond, published for health and social workers and counsellors (Richman 1993). Another vital support is for adults to be able to share their anxieties with their colleagues so that they can plan helpful responses together.

Because of these anxieties, as shown in the next example, when these are assumed to be routine and inevitable, children's distress and their protests can pass unrecognised, until they are shown in a new light, as in a film. The example also shows how painful it can be for adults to hear children's protests, and to accept them to the extent of questioning and then changing their own policies.

Laura

Films of distressed young children in children's homes and hospitals 40 years ago (Robertson and Robertson 1989), led to great changes which could be said to have followed the voice of the child. Parents gradually came to be encouraged to stay with their child in hospital, and when children in care had to be separated from their parents, social workers made greater efforts to provide more consistent and personal care for them.

One doctor described his pain on watching a film about two-year-old Laura, made with his permission on his own ward (MacCarthy 1979). At first he could not bear to believe that his well-intentioned policy of banning parents from the ward, because they were thought to upset children, could distress the children so much, and he dismissed the idea. Then the ward sister said that the film made her see everything in a new light and she was determined to change the policy, so he agreed, and became a leading advocate for welcoming parents into children's wards.

Recent reanalysis of the Robertsons' films questions the assumption that young children are inevitably distressed in a new setting without their parents (Barrett 1998). John and Laura initially react quite calmly and stoically and try to adapt. It is only when their efforts to establish relationships with the staff are repeatedly denied, and when Laura has had surgery, that they become more and more distressed. This suggests that young children can have reserves of confidence and willingness to adapt and take part in their new setting, if adults expect them to, and treat them as, reasonable partners, not simply as helpless dependents. This also involves recognising how the children can be among each others' greatest asset and friends. One difference found between nurseries where children are very distressed and ones where they are much happier is that in the first type children tend to be slotted in at different times of the day with different groups of children. In the second type they attend sessions regularly, get to know the routine and, most importantly, are able to enjoy close continuing friendships with other children (Penn 1997a, 1998b).

Prejudice that it is not worthwhile to talk or listen to young children

This is the greatest barrier, and once it is overcome, the rewards of talking with children can help to resolve all the other barriers.

METHODS OF TALKING WITH YOUNG CHILDREN

The next two sections mention a few of the books on this topic, rather than repeating the information given by them. A major resource is the practical books about play and games which extend ways of consulting and working closely with young children, for example, those published by the National Early Years Network and Save the Children. Careful working together is emphasised, for example, in *Never Too Young* (Miller 1997). This book about the early years lists the steps adults and children can take together; their manner of talking together – sitting on an equal level, not interrupting, being honest, acknowledging feelings, adults not asking questions when children expect adults already to know the answers. The book describes practical techniques, games and creative activities, through which young children have serious discussions.

An Eye for an Eye Leaves Everyone Blind (Finch 1998) also gives practical ways of working and playing with young children to resolve conflict, to listen, share and negotiate. There is a section on monitoring and review, which lists ways of checking how different approaches do or do not work over time. Children are asked which ones make them happy or unhappy, and adults check signs of progress such as 'time out' and other sanctions being used less often.

Books about babies communicating with adults and with one another show how early in life they begin to express themselves through their voices and bodies, to share, to join and leave a group, to lead and follow, create rituals for greetings and farewells (Goldschmeid and Selleck 1996) and, for example, share milk bottles as tokens of friendship (Whaley and Rubenstein 1994) and become disturbed if they see another baby is distressed (Eisenberg 1992, p.199).

Empowering Children and Young People: A Training Manual for Promoting Involvement in Decision-making (Treseder 1997) is about eight-year-olds plus, but makes many points about consulting groups and individuals of any age. The book covers ways that children can manage consultations: chairing a meeting well; welcoming people; agreeing the agenda; thinking about timing; using play for breaks and energisers to keep people's interest and enthusiasm; breaking up into smaller groups during meetings; using short clear words; having pre-meetings to help new people see more clearly what is going on; and ensuring that everyone understands each new point. There are exercises for young people and adults to increase their skill and cooperation. Consultation is seen as a long-term process in which each person gradually becomes more skilled, and groups develop long-standing methods, rather than quick one-off attempts. Slowly, people learn to share responsibility, to overcome barriers, and find which methods work best for them. The book has lists of barriers, tools and skills, and shows what can be gained when things go wrong. Groups of any age 'storm, form and norm' while they work through disagreements and while people with different temperaments get to know and trust one another. This process must be allowed for, if groups are not to give up consulting in the early stages.

The planning tree

An example of a method used with teenagers is the planning tree when in small groups they draw a large tree trunk, and talk about: 'What can we do?' Then they write the agreed aims on the trunk. They talk about whom they want to affect, and put the four main types of people on short branches. Then they talk about the good things they want to achieve with the help of these people, and write these on coloured cards to put on the branches. They talk about the bad effects that might happen, and finally about neutral or non-effects, again on coloured cards. The patterns formed by the tree help them to look ahead and put several ideas, which they may already be thinking about, into a helpful order and balance. Young children on school councils might use the tree when solving a problem or planning an activity (Treseder 1997).

The books emphasise that a vital part of consulting children is to respect their decisions. After long, careful discussion, for the staff to say, 'we would like to do what you want but we can't afford it' can be worse than not consulting children at all. It is necessary to explain any financial or other limitations while talking with children. Young children can understand about costs and budgeting.

Talking about budgets

Some children aged two to four years were given a budget of £30, represented by 30 discs, and a toyshop catalogue. They talked about which toys they would choose for their group to have and, with some adult help, they matched their 'money' to the toys they chose. 'They were able to consider the needs of the group as a whole, negotiate with each other, and choose a range of toys that were sensible, good buys' (Miller 1999).

If there is not enough money, say for an outing to the seaside, the children may invent an alternative such as making their own beach (Mepani and Emerson 1998).

MAKING PERSONAL DECISIONS

It can be easier for health and social work professionals working with individual children to share in making decisions with them, than for play and education staff caring for large groups and having to balance different children's interests. Yet, as just shown, young children can negotiate and share in groups, and doing so is an important part of their lives and learning.

Social workers have to consult the individuals they care for (Department of Health 1989); however, children may not be informed properly before or during meetings and may be daunted by the adults attending. Informing, preparing and supporting children though the whole process of consultation, especially involves these five aspects (Hodgson 1995):

- access to those with power – it is no use junior staff talking to children unless they can ensure that their reasonable requests can be met;
- being provided with relevant information, before, during and after being consulted. In at least some social services departments children are discouraged from attending court hearings ('you'll be bored' – as if their life chances do not matter) and they may not be told until weeks later a decision about where they will live (Masson and Winn 1999);

- genuine choice between distinctive options, not trivial choices like 'we're moving you on, do you want to go by bus or by train?' (Gardner 1989);

- a trusted independent person to give support and be a representative if needed, with the child having some choice in who this person is; and

- a means of redress for appeal or complaint.

METHODS OF RESEARCH WITH CHILDREN

Points made in the previous section about practical communication are also useful in research with and by children. In all kinds of settings, children use simple research methods: talking, making a list or a few drawings to summarise the options they have described, and then voting for their most-or-least-liked option by putting a mark, or a sticker or stone by their chosen items. Some groups choose from a set of pictures, or select a sad or happy face to express their response. Some groups use art equipment, make masks or puppets, create dramas and stories and collages to record their experiences, hopes or plans. Some make maps, for example, of their daily round of collecting firewood and animals' food in Nepal (Johnson, Hill and Ivan-Smith 1995), or an ecology map of birds sighted in Canada (Hart 1997). Some use cameras, tape recorders, survey sheets or video cameras. A comprehensive and very practical review of methods is in *Children in Focus* (Boyden and Ennew 1997). Methods developed with rather than on adults who have little education or rights, through participatory appraisal, paved the way for children to become more involved too (Pratt and Loizos 1992).

Children's Childhoods Observed and Experienced (Mayall 1994b), *Research with Children* (Christensen and James 2000), and *Stepping Forward* (Johnson *et al.* 1998) are all international collections which discuss research methods partly in the context of children's rights. *Listening to Children: Ethics and Social Research* (Alderson 1995) reviews the legal and ethical background to consulting children, and includes ten topics to help adults to check the standards of their work with children in relation to:

- the purpose of the work;

- possible costs and benefits;

- respecting privacy and confidentiality;

- decisions about which children to involve or exclude;
- funding;
- planning and revising research aims and methods;
- informing the children and adults concerned;
- consent;
- reporting and using the findings; and
- the possible impact on children.

On the final point, much is written about the impact on children, and protecting and respecting them, during research and other consultation, but little is written on the likely after-effects of research reports, possibly on millions of other children. For example, research is often quoted to 'prove' how vulnerable and dependent all children are. *Listening to Children* suggests how researchers can take account of the potential impact on all children of their published reports, and can try to ensure that their conclusions are firmly based in the evidence. Researchers respect children's worth and dignity by using positive images, avoiding discrimination, and enabling children to speak directly, in their own terms (Save the Children n.d.).

INTERPRETING EVIDENCE AND RESPONDING TO CHILDREN'S VIEWS

Once children have expressed views, there can be further challenges in deciding how to interpret and respond to them. Even when children appear to be talking directly, as in a television programme, it is vital to check how adults may be shaping children's responses. For example, they may confine children's responses to simple issues, and edit out longer words and more complex ideas (Thornborrow 1998). Research material which seems to support an obvious conclusion may have another explanation.

The book corner

Researchers showed children photographs of each main area of their family centre. They asked the children which areas they liked best and least. The book area was the least popular place (Miller 1998).

This example might be seen as evidence of children's immaturity and the need for adults to ensure that the book corner was well used. It could also be seen as a prompt to improve the books. However, through observing and listening as well as asking direct questions, the researchers concluded that some children disliked the way the book corner was used – to keep them quiet and constrained, and for reading stories to large groups. The family centre staff and children tried new ways of using the book corner and other areas more freely, and of having smaller story groups.

It is vital to ask wary, critical questions about the process of consulting at every stage of research, and to examine how the context, methods and relationships might shape the replies. Heather saying 'no' in Chapter 2 illustrates how a seemingly obvious interpretation might be a misunderstanding. Examining *why* people think and speak the way they do, their reasoning and values, as well as their yes/no replies, is important.

QUALITY AND QUANTITY IN RESEARCH

Most research measures children. The reports emphasise numbers, tables and graphs, standardised questions and tests, and representative samples in controlled or laboratory conditions. Yet all these methods tend to find lower abilities in children than 'naturally'-occurring observations discover, when researchers interact flexibly with children, and respond to each child's concerns as well as to common factors across groups. The leading researcher Judy Dunn commented: 'Young children's logical capacities in *conversation* are considerably greater than those reported in test situations' (Dunn 1995). Children in a representative sample are inevitably far less knowledgeable than those selected for their relevant experience. For instance, children with serious illness know much more about illness and treatment (Alderson 1993) than an average group of children will know (Grisso and Vierling 1978). So how wise or ignorant children are assumed to be in certain matters very much depends on which kinds of children are selected for the research.

Much also depends on the research method. New understandings of babies' immense capacities, which contradict traditional and still dominant research conclusions, come from extremely-detailed sensitive research with a few children in their own everyday settings. It is impossible to do such intensive and contextual research with large numbers of children.

Yet the 'hard' methods of larger surveys to support 'scientific' generalisations remain more popular and generally respected than 'softer' approaches like conversations or video-taped observations. Numbers are very important in large-scale measurements and general-isations, such as numbers of children living in poverty. But numbers can be unhelpful when researching children's capacities. It does not matter if a few or many very young babies engage in long interactions with one another, or how many six-year-olds share in making decisions about their major surgery, or how many children are extremely distressed if they are smacked. The point is that *some* of them clearly have this capacity. And knowing this opens the way for adults to be more aware of all children's potential, and to search with each child how much he or she can understand and be involved, instead of assuming incapacity.

Qualitative research takes a rainbow approach, exploring the differ-ences in each child and circumstance, enlarging understanding and empathy. Quantitative research takes a binary black and white ap-proach, in order to classify and count similarities. It can be as dangerous and misleading to over-generalise from 2,000 children as from two. Qualitative and quantitative methods can both be used well or badly, appropriately or inappropriately, depending on the kinds of questions and data concerned.

Part of the challenge for researchers who discover unexpected abilities in young children is to gain respect for the qualitative methods they need to use, as well as for their findings. Some critics find fault with the methods used, as an excuse to dismiss disturbing and challenging findings. A usual device is to argue that the research involves too few children. However, criticisms about numbers may really express pol-itical and emotional reservations, the deeper feelings discussed in Chapter 3. Instead of being side-tracked into (often ignorant) argu-ments about research methods, it may be more useful to discuss research politics, whether the critics are worried that emancipatory research findings might offend influential supporters and funders, and if so, why they are worried (for connections between research methods and politics, see Alderson 1998).

PUBLISHING AND DISSEMINATING

Much research remains unpublished, which lets down the children and adults who contributed data, the research team, the funders, and everyone who might benefit from the findings. Critical reports and 'negative findings', which show that a technique or system does not work well, are especially liable not to be published. Yet they can be vital in helping to stop useless or harmful practices, and in speaking for young children whose difficulties or suffering may otherwise pass unrecognised. To avoid the serious problem of non-publication, it is useful to have a multi-disciplinary advisory group willing to defend the project publicly if necessary, and also to sort out clearly agreed and recorded publishing plans and copyrights in advance (NCB 1993).

Disseminating goes beyond publishing. It means sowing seeds and, more than getting a report into people's hands, it is getting the ideas into their minds and hearts, by helping them to become intellectually convinced and emotionally committed to the conclusions. Bridging the difficult gaps between research, policy and practice is helped when researchers meet policy-makers and practitioners half way to discuss how links might be made, without dictating how they should be made. Teenage researchers are very conscious of this crucial task. They tend to begin their projects by talking about whom they want to influence, and how, and what kinds of research will help to achieve these aims (Alan Siddall, Save the Children, personal communication).

CHAPTER FIVE

Levels of Young Children's Involvement

Beyond the individual level, of adults and children working in pairs and small groups, how can children's views influence policies at a wider level – in local communities, nationally and internationally? Also, at what levels, in relation to the degree of involvement, do young children take part in influencing and making decisions? Are children used by adults, or at least informed by them, or are they more fully consulted, or do they take a leading part in projects? This chapter considers these questions.

AT THE LOCAL LEVEL

Working mainly with small groups of disadvantaged children, researchers have shown how skilful children can be when they are involved in giving evidence and in working as co-researchers. Researchers have written detailed reports of their findings and their methods (Boyden and Ennew 1997): the funding, ethics and access; how children and adults together design research methods; topics and questions; numerous ways of collecting data; and their discussions about what the data mean and how they can be reported; and how to work with authorities to see that the findings are understood and used. The reports include work in the UK by, for example, teenagers leaving local authority care, and children living on deprived housing estates, who are involved at various stages of the research (Howarth 1997; Wellard, Tearse and West 1997; West 1995). Most of those involved are teenagers, and far less is known yet about the views of younger children such as being looked after by local authorities (Thomas 1998) and the decisions they would like to share in making when their parents separate (O'Quigley 1999). Yet some projects include people aged eight years upwards, and some of the older ones research young children's views. Participation Education Group involved 187 of their members aged five to twenty-five in a survey for their report on how schools can seriously damage your health (PEG 1997). Another local project, research about a housing estate by preschool-age children was mentioned in the Introduction to this book.

AT THE LOCAL AUTHORITY LEVEL

Inspired by the UN Convention on the Rights of the Child, the report *Hear! Hear!* (Willow 1997) reviews many good examples of involving some of the almost 13 million people aged up to eighteen years in the UK in commenting and advising about local authorities' services. The book includes assessments about what consultation methods do or do not work well, and the strong arguments for involving children. There are, for example, the Langley Children's Forum, Rochdale, which involves people aged five to fourteen; Kids' Count, where the Newcastle Victoria Infirmary responds to children's views (Cunliffe and English 1997); and Derby Children's Hospital, designed with the help of 130 people aged six to sixteen in workshops. The Derby architect said: 'It makes our job a lot easier ... now we know what they want ... this is their building', such as with the lower reception desk which children can see over when they check themselves in.

Hampshire Social Services asked foster carers' own children for their views, which were quite positive, until they were asked to complete the sentence 'When a foster child leaves I feel ...'. The children replied 'I feel relieved' which made social workers more concerned about their feelings, so that they now attend more to this group as well as to the fostered children.

In a research project over two years, health visitors in Tower Hamlets worked with four to six year olds, and found they disliked: cockroaches; dogs; dirty noisy streets; grassy areas because they had broken glass, dog dirt and rubbish; and the lack of trees, flowers and play areas. The adults reported; 'This project has clearly demonstrated that even children as young as four are able to communicate how they feel.'

In Greenwich, people aged eight to nineteen advised on the Borough's anti-poverty strategy and showed the value of consulting people of different age groups with different experiences of being excluded, with many valuable ideas coming to light. Over five years, several London Boroughs are consulting 4,500 people aged seven to seventeen on regeneration. As *Hear! Hear!* (Willow 1997) comments, careful planning, clear targets and outcomes with time scales are vital, which the London project has with the support of senior officials.

When children in Kirkholt, Rochdale, were consulted about improving their neighbourhood, using a 12–foot scaled model of the area, a seven-year-old asked: 'But how will we know when things have happened?' So the Council keeps in touch with the children, reports progress, and returns to consult them at each new stage.

From one authority, the Redbridge report (which included the book-corner survey mentioned earlier (NEYN/Redbridge LA 1998)), gives details about:

- the advantages and disadvantages of using outside consultants, and the value of using them to pass on their skills to the staff;

- the principles of a successful consultation, such as being positive;

- the need to agree on clear plans, timescale, and resource allocation including cover for staff involved in the project;

- plans for staff training, and for informing everyone affected by the project, before, during and afterwards – this may mean writing to some adults and children individually if messages are not passed on to them;

- the necessary commitment of the adults concerned to listen respectfully and to act on the findings;

- the flexible methods of varied meetings, interviews, surveys and observations used;

and the detailed encounters and findings.

There are also many reports about children's views of, and place in, the family (Beck 1997; CRO 1995b), in child care (Cumber 1989; Goldschmeid 1989; Beardsley 1990; Daycare Trust n.d.; Abbott and Moylett 1997; Bawden et al. 1997), in early years centres and schools (Cullingford 1992; David 1992; ACE 1995; Curtis 1996; David 1996; Ensing 1996; Fisher 1996; Giller and Tisdall 1997; Whalley 1998); and about how the UN Convention 1989 can inform local authorities (AMA/CRO 1995; CRO 1995a) and health services (EACH 1993; British Association for Child Health 1995) and link social services and health care (Audit Commission 1994).

The Office of Children's Rights Commissioner for London (a post created in 2000) will promote respect for the views of London's 1.4 million children in all aspects of London government: this should make London an exemplary child-friendly city.

AT THE NATIONAL LEVEL

Forty-five groups of people aged five to eighteen years were asked about how they thought the authorities were meeting the standards set out in the Convention, and their views are quoted throughout a national report on all kinds of evidence on how children's rights are respected in the UK (Lansdown and Newell 1994). This report was presented to the UN Committee on the Rights of the Child when the Committee also received the official UK Government report in 1995.

For the year 2000 report, the Government consulted much more widely and paid for Save the Children to consult with 40 groups of children, 400 in all, aged four to seventeen years. The groups discussed many aspects of the Convention, and prepared the children's report (Save the Children 1999), launched at the House of Commons in May 1999. The non-governmental organisations also submitted a report to the UN Committee.

The report *Effective Government Structures for Children* (Hodgkin and Newell 1996) calls for national changes to enable central government to be more responsive to the needs and rights of children across the UK. These include: child impact and budget analyses of the effects directly on children (not just on families or schools) of all government policies: routine methods of consulting children and promoting their active participation; annual reports on the state of UK children; closer liaison between all government departments about how they affect children; a children's rights commissioner; and other changes which go right to the heart of government in the cabinet office.

Most reports are about consulting children individually and in small groups, and their views about how national policies affect them are little known. In debates on the government initiatives, such as Meeting the Child Care Challenge and Welfare to Work, designed to increase the income of young families through organising child care so that parents can do paid work, children's voices and coordinated policy starting from their views are missing (Moss and Petrie 1997).

Nationally, young children are being ever more closely organised through English schools. Four-year-olds follow the national curriculum, the daily literacy hour and, from autumn 1999, the maths 40 minutes, and they have SATs (Standard Attainment Tests) and OFSTED inspections with the pressures on staff and pupils to perform well. Play areas are disappearing from infant school classrooms, and play times are being cut or cancelled (Blatchford 1998). Teachers are advised to use formal instruction methods with narrow ability groups, and activities that can be tested, rather than shared discovery and creative work in mixed groups. From autumn 1999, parents were invited to sign home-school agreements promising regular and punctual attendance, good discipline and behaviour and homework (DfEE 1998b). These do not allow for children's reasonable reactions to things they are unhappy about at school, and are the opposite of real contracts which are specific agreements between fairly equal, informed and unpressured people or groups based on mutual consultation (Save the Children 1999, pp.10–12). School governors do not have to consult pupils when each school designs its own contract. Governors are left to decide whether 'the pupils concerned are sufficiently mature to understand the contents of the agreement'. It is not clear what is the point of parents making promises, such as about their child's future behaviour, if the child is seen as unable to understand the promise.

The home-school agreements, with homework for all children, extend school discipline into the home, further limiting children's freedoms. Parents have to pay for some kinds of after-school clubs but not for homework clubs, leading to confusing debates about what counts as homework, and why. Children's views on the different settings and activities need to be heard, if assessments of their effects are to be realistic (Black 1991).

AT THE INTERNATIONAL LEVEL

The UN Committee on the Rights of the Child hears regular reports from governments on their progress in implementing the Convention. Reports from governments, and more critical reports from non-governmental organisations, are making up a growing body of evidence about children's lives which include some reports from children. The Convention works as a tool for consulting children about every aspect of their lives, in order to improve ways of implementing the Convention using their knowledge (Ennew 1997; European Commission 1996).

One international organisation has been initiated by street children who are campaigning for better conditions (see the whole special issue of *Childhood 3*, 2, including Bemak 1996; Ennew and Connolly 1996). Since 1992 EcoCity has enabled young children to research and present their views about their city to councillors. Given enough time and resources, this can have 'valuable and significant outcomes ... adults are always amazed and impressed at children's ability to understand complex issues such as city infrastructure and their realistic suggestions about how to improve their local and global environment, and to consider other needs, rights and responsibilities' (Willow 1997). There are plans for an international children's parliament. As global communications and networks grow, international associations for children and teenagers are also likely to increase. One fast-growing method is through email and website contacts, which overcome many of the costs and other problems of travel and needing escorts for children.

GENERAL POINTS

Most of the reports mentioned here discuss why it is important to consult children, the barriers to doing so, and ways around these. There are limitations in over-individualising children's responses and not relating them to broader political contexts. One way to address this huge and neglected area of children speaking at national and international levels is: through overviews and cooperation between many smaller projects; to see how they complement or contradict one another, and why; to see how gaps might be filled; and how research and practice reports could be coordinated to support more general recommendations based on children's views and experiences. For example, the Redbridge enquiry (NEYN/Redbridge LA 1998) involved over 70 children aged from two to eight years across the Borough. Among the outcomes, pre-school centres have started new listening methods and times, and schools are using the children's ideas on helping new children to settle into school, on dealing with bullying, improving a school map and resolving problems in dinner queues.

Another approach is to devise methods of large-scale enquiry among young children to complement smaller in-depth studies. The questionnaire booklet mentioned earlier, which divided children's participation rights into topics which concern children at school and asked them for their views, in simple sections, is one such example (Alderson 1999). Over 2,500 young people replied aged from seven to seventeen years. Younger children could take part more in such mass surveys developed with their help, and completed individually and in small groups, working with someone older to read and write for them.

The first national government-funded programme of research about children's own views (1996–2000) concentrated on the ages five to sixteen. It is convincing researchers how worthwhile it is to consult children and to work with 'user' organisations as they are encouraged to do (ESRC 1996). In time, this may be followed by a similar programme on birth to eight year olds.

LEVELS OF PARTICIPATION

Besides the levels of scale, there are also different levels of degrees of participation when children and adults work together, as reviewed in this section. One of the first to be published was Arnstein's ladder (Arnstein 1969).

Arnstein's ladder of participation

1. Manipulation – pretending to consult.

2. Therapy – talking which does not lead to any change.

3. Information – from those in authority.

4. Consultation – but not necessarily with any active results.

5. Placation – seeming to change and involve people more but with no real effects.

6. Partnership – sharing planning and decision-making.

7. Delegated power – citizens share control and bargain with officials.

8. Citizens control – through routine programmes.

At the first levels, people may be exploited against their will or interests. The pretence of being involved can be worse than being excluded. At higher levels, people share power more equally, and at the highest level citizens or service users are free to develop their own concerns. This ladder was devised for adult citizens and takes an American model of democracy and liberty.

Roger Hart's ladder (Hart 1992) suits schools and nurseries more, though it is criticised as too cautious, to adult-centric, and too concerned with adults' bestowing opportunities to participate on to children (Franklin 1995).

Hart's ladder of participation

1. Manipulation.
2. Decoration – like children singing at adult conferences.
3. Tokenism – such as children being used to seem to rubber-stamp adults decisions.
4. Assigned but not informed.
5. Consulted and informed.
6. Adult-initiated, shared decisions with children.
7. Child-initiated and directed.
8. Child-initiated, shared decisions with adults.

There is some disagreement over whether children are most emancipated when they act independently or with adults. When young children have information and support from adults, they are more likely to be able to negotiate informed decisions and to solve problems. One example is the preschool group of children who planned a menu working to a budget, went shopping and cooked the meal together, with some adult help (Miller 1997). As with the dinosaur project in Chapter 2, this shows the benefits of children having time and space to share their own ways of creating and of solving problems, without needing adults to intervene. Current millennium awards schemes recognise: 'that working with young people is constantly changing and developing, and we must develop new models of good practice to...add to our power to influence' (Save the Children 1998). Here, the ladder is seen as:

E) child initiated and directed
D) child initiated, shared decisions
C) adult initiated, shared decisions
B) consulted and informed
A) assigned but informed

The ladders are perhaps useful, not so much as markers to measure progress up the levels, but as ways of clarifying and checking how much children are involved in each part of a project, and how much more they might be involved depending on what is practical and effective. Children and adults may disagree about the assessments and need to discuss them. Groups often work at several different levels of the ladder at once. Another way of clarifying degrees of participation is to divide them simply into two types. Latent participation is having a share or a stake in activities, taking part almost by default. Active participation means being actively involved at all levels of decision-making, having a real say, and children are quickly aware of tokenism and being 'played like fools' (Morrow 1999). As adults and young children gain experience, confidence and expertise in working together more actively, higher and wider (national and international) levels of participation are likely to be achieved.

CHAPTER 6

Consulting Young Children
Through Work and Play

One frequent theme in reports about consulting young children is balancing play and work, an important theme which has its own short chapter here. Questions arise about who is working or playing, and the contribution of play while consulting and researching with young children. Involving people, when it is fun and interesting for all concerned, can encourage imaginative creativity and enjoyment in shared projects, as well as enthusiasm for the aims they might achieve. This chapter reviews how work and play mix, or are distinct from one another, and what play means.

THE EXAMPLE OF VIDEOS

Making videos enables children to express their experiences very directly. Yet the more elaborate and intriguing the equipment, the more the children may want to play and experiment with it, rather than using it as a tool to respond to adults' questions. Brazilian children acted to the video camera, which they were not allowed to hold, as if they were playing grand parts in a play which frustrated the researchers who wanted the children to respond more 'naturally' (Faulkner 1998).

When presented with a new gadget such as a video camera, some people read the handbook or ask an expert for help, other people of all ages 'play around' with it, discovering and inventing imaginatively for themselves how to use it and how it works. Some children first use a video camera by playing around like this, and in time they might create the most interesting films, as long as time is allowed for them to reach that stage. One project reported the probably frequent experience of adults who work with children on a more equal basis. This project suggested that the children preferred not to express themselves in writing, but used video and Polaroid cameras as powerful tools to express their strong views (F. Smith 1998). An example is that one group disliked the term 'after-school club' and they renamed their club as 'the crystal palace'.

When new equipment is used while consulting with children, it is important to allow enough time for them to play with it, if they want to, before using it for the consultation, and to see all their responses as useful parts of the consultation. If there is not time to play experimentally, then it may be better to use familiar or more simple tools.

Other fairly elaborate equipment is not necessarily helpful. When young children were consulted about new playground plans, they tended to say 'yes' to everything which the attractive puppets asked them, and to run under the parachute because they liked doing that rather than to express a view. Later the questioners resorted to asking children simply to point to the pictures of equipment they preferred (Newson 1995b).

FOCUS GROUPS

Children's responses vary, depending on the setting, size of groups, methods and attitudes of the researchers. This can happen with all age groups. Focus groups are supposed to generate new ideas through the interactions between all members of the group. This involves having conversations rather more like everyday talk, instead of stilted replies to set questions. In any group, however, if the talk is ordinary, then it will be rather chaotic and interrupted – some researchers see this as successful group work, others as their failure to control.

Consulting in groups: Between control and chaos

In focus groups about children's views of violence (M. Smith 1998), the girls cooperated with the researchers and tried to keep order and repair interruptions which the boys kept making. The boys tried to stay on the edges of the talk, and joined in rather disruptively as if they were interested but wanted to keep their independence and not fit in neatly with the adults' plans. The researchers were pleased with these revealing responses, and felt that the boys were joining in on their own terms, and that the aim to encourage everyday free talk worked well – despite problems with transcribing the audio-tapes.

PLAYING AND WORKING

Adults sometimes give mixed messages to children. 'We're going to play some games and have fun doing this,' a play worker might say, when she wants to find out their views on bullying. If the children respond by playing around and enjoying themselves, the adults worry that the balance between serious consulting and fun has gone wrong. This is partly because play has conflicting meanings.

Play has been described as the child's work or language. Adults use play with a purpose to educate children, to assess their physical, cognitive and emotional development, to help them to practise for their adult future, and to occupy and control them gently but firmly. In contrast, to many children, this kind of play is too much mixed with duty. For them, play is freedom from adult control, spontaneously doing as they like *because* they enjoy that, and for no other reason, an especially precious time which they rarely have. Many adults find this free play worrying and threatening, if it seems to border on danger or conflict, seems too noisy or too much like time-wasting nonsense. However, other adults see this as real play, a complex 'unfolding narrative' (Mayles 1989; Strandell 2000), which children organise themselves if given the chance. In this second view, notions of 'poor quality' or 'inappropriate' play are contradictions in terms if play is valued for itself. Whereas adults tend to use play for other purposes, children see play as an end in itself. For adults, play is about developing the (future) self; for children, play is often about being in (present) relationships (Holdigan 2000).

Conflicts between adults' and children's meanings of play are increased when the adults begin a session on consulting children by emphasising the fun and play aspects. Adults may be vague about the consultation purposes, for fear of boring, confusing or deterring the children. If the children respond by playing at tasks they have been set, which are not very relevant to the consultation, the adults may then assume that children cannot be consulted – before they have tried asking them directly.

Other adult meanings of play include pretend play, and play as an escape from harsh reality and the pressures of real life. Play used as a diversion by consulters during breaks and energizers – games to renew children's enthusiasm – fits this view of play as fantasy, which children are used to adults assuming. However, if the consulting involves real serious work, to affect present realities, and not simply to practise for the future, then it is confusing to mix it too much with play.

Almost all the work which children and teenagers do – housework, babysitting, washing a car, weekend work in a shop – is not seen as real work but as practising for adulthood (Morrow 1994), opportunities which adults provide for children. The play worker quoted on page 15, who said he was used to 'working' with young children but was amazed to find that he could consult them, expresses this assumed split between working adults and playful children. Consulting involves partly closing this split, and working on a serious equal level. When consulting is too playful, it is harder for adults and children to see their more equal status and shared serious purpose.

The same activity might be called play when children do it and work when adults do it, like making the dinosaur models (Chapter 2). The English language does not have a word for activity which is serious, challenging, maybe difficult, enjoyable, amusing, fun, entertaining, and rewarding both in itself and for other reasons. When adults plan to consult young children seriously, they need to decide if they plan to use playful methods, and if so which kinds and why.

Play can complement work and is useful in several ways to effective consultation. People of all ages can work more intensely and closely together when they also enjoy playful ice-breakers, and activities which mix fun with effort. By laughing together they may become more relaxed, open, trusting, and attentive.

PLAY AND RESEARCH

Play methods are integral to some methods of consulting children.

The naughty teddy

One of the most important scientific studies with young children was done with a 'naughty teddy'. Psychologists had been led to believe that young children's thinking is inconsistent and confused because, in tests devised by Piaget and replicated around the world, when they were asked the same question several times, they tended to vary their answers. It seems that the children assumed that researchers wanted a different answer each time the children were asked a question, but when the children tried to be helpful, researchers assumed that they could not think consistently. However, when asked the same questions by the teddy, the children laughed at his repetitions and firmly repeated their original answers. They did not feel they had to be polite to the teddy or pretend not to notice his curious repetitions (Donaldson 1978).

Similarly, researchers asking children about smacking enquired through Splodge, an ignorant visitor from another planet, so avoiding the problem of asking the children questions to which children would expect adults already to know the answers (Willow and Hyder 1998).

Researchers planning to interview children aged from eight years about how much they felt they were involved in decisions about their major surgery decided to use hospital play sets and art work. The aims were to help children to express themselves and to help them (and perhaps the researchers) to feel relaxed and comfortable when talking about stressful topics (Alderson 1993). However, the children were not interested in toys, they wanted to be interviewed as they had seen people talking on television. Many seemed very pleased to have a chance to tell their story. Some children with severe learning difficulties also very much enjoy talking into a tape recorder (Alderson and Goodey 1998).

Play methods can tap children's imagination. Talking about 'let's pretend' can involve young children in planning improvements in playgrounds and nurseries. One lively, well-illustrated pack produced with children shows how to promote genuine participation, negotiation and power sharing (Save the Children/Kirklees 1996). The play approaches help research teams to enjoy being together as well as working together. There are details on promoting equal opportunities and 'chat space methods'.

Yet instead of assuming that play is the only language and method through which to work with young children, consulters could decide what kinds of play, if any, might be useful, and why, and with whom. Otherwise, children may feel used and not properly consulted, either over the methods they are expected to work with, or about the purpose of the consulting. They may want to opt out but feel that they can only refuse indirectly, by not cooperating. Then, the adults' methods of consulting will contradict their purposes of listening and respecting. Work and play often overlap, but there are times when one or other is most appropriate, and consulting young children involves 'working out' with them when this is so (Kefyalew 1996).

CHAPTER SEVEN

Risk and Control, Conflict and Violence

Some of the main complications when consulting children are adults' concerns about risk, and potential loss of control, conflict and violence, and doubts about when adults should be in sole control or share responsibilities with young children.

RISK AND CONTROL

> **John, Susan, Roger and Titty**, aged 7 to 12 years, asked their parents if they could go off sailing and camping on their own in the Lake District for three weeks. Their naval officer father sent a telegram giving permission by saying: 'Better drowned than duffers, if not duffers, won't drown' (Ransome 1930).

Although this is a fictional example, and exciting children's books have somehow to remove the parents in Chapter 1, it illustrates the great change in beliefs about reasonable risks over the past few decades in the UK. Matters on which children can be consulted and trusted are in many ways more limited today than they have ever been, because of fears about risk and control. There never was a golden age of respecting children, but in the past working-class children tended to be left alone more by adults in their free time to play in the streets and countryside.

Concern about risk reduces the scope for consulting children. The examples of William Blake, Albert, Margaret and Kevin earlier show how beliefs about reasonable risk vary greatly. They are influenced, for instance, by the rise in car use, so that in Britain, whereas in 1971 80 per cent of seven to eight-year-olds went to school on their own, by 1990 only nine per cent did (Hillman, Adams and Whiteleg 1990). This cuts down the way young children can express views, such as a wish to walk around the town alone. Adults do not offer choices which they feel they must veto. A young child out alone in an English street today tends to be seen with pity, and concern about parents' negligence, not as an ordinary pedestrian like Albert or Margaret (in the Introduction). It is as if the streets in the UK now belong to adults as well as the roads.

Children are treated and seen, by adults and by themselves, as dependent and vulnerable when they do not have the chance to be independent. Through lack of opportunity they are less competent and confident. Whereas children used to play in large groups in the streets in 1900, now they are a much smaller part of the population, they live further apart, and there are many more only children. If they want to see friends, their parents often have to telephone to arrange a meeting, and escort them there. As in the past, when children have to ask adults' permission about many aspects of their lives, this can reinforce adults' beliefs that adults should decide matters such as when children eat or sleep, what they wear or read, when they go out or stay at home, without necessarily consulting children's views.

Traffic is only part of the problem. There is also the fear of stranger-danger, increased by frequent media stories which perpetuate vulnerable child images. For example, on the day these words are being written, every national newspaper's front pages carries reports about two lost and found ten-year-olds in Hastings. Commentators are calling for teachers and parents to check more closely on where every child is each morning. The way children are increasingly excluded from public spaces leads to a stray child now being seen as far more (negligently) isolated than when children once filled the streets, and almost being seen as fair game by molesters. These newly-constructed dangers and losses to children's lives of freedom to roam and to meet together in public spaces are seldom mentioned to balance the arguments about protecting them. Yet if children do not learn to mix freely and to support one another, they are left much more vulnerable. Children's views on how their lives are restricted, and the risks of confining them into 'home-school-car' are rarely heard publicly.

British parents are expected to worry if their child is late and to arrange adult care after school whereas, children in Norway and Finland enjoy being at home without their parents from about seven years upwards (Solberg 1997). Norwegian children have more hours away from adult supervision, and a slightly higher accident rate than other European children, which the Norwegians consider is worth risking for the benefits of freely enjoying the countryside (Frönes 1994). There is not a public fear of stranger-danger in Scandinavia. Finnish children start school at seven years, and on some days go home at 11 am where they play with friends until their parents arrive home in the late afternoon, often after dark. In some other countries, adults supervise every hour of the child's day with school and homework from four years of age, and other formal sessions for music or sports. This raises the questions: Whom does childhood belong to when their time and space are organised around adults' priorities about children's best interests? And how much say can and should children have in daily choices? (Lorenzo 1992; Shamgar-Handleman 1994).

A decision which seems cautious to one person can look dangerous to another, and adults tend to be more cautious when caring for other people's children partly in case the parent is very cautious, partly because of fairly new ideas about risk. Increasingly, risk is not simply the chance of slight harm to the child, but of all the possible dangers which might occur and should be prevented. Adults also fear risks to their own reputation, and being disciplined, sacked, sued or criticised in the newspapers if a child is harmed. In a risk-conscious society, accidents are believed not to exist, someone must always be found to blame (Green 1997). Risk management transfers greater responsibility on to adults and more dependency on to children, as shown by the contrast between children's holidays in the 1900s and the 1930s in the earlier sailing example.

SCHOOL EDUCATION FOR FUTURE PARENTS AND CARERS

The first page of Helena's GCSE child care file shows the two-year curriculum. The course had three main themes: equipment, safety and food. The equipment section covered many items which babies and young children are supposed to need: clothes, cots and prams, baby chairs and travelling bags, trikes and slides. Pictures of these were cut from catalogues and neatly stuck into pages of notes. The play and activity sections emphasised, besides the required toys, the vital need to keep children safe from accidents, infection and any other dangers, they must be constantly cleaned and guarded. Their slow cognitive development, set out in mile stones, is shown to prevent them from being responsible.

The food sections were filled with leaflets from firms which provide many kinds of refined food and drink, on the nutritional value of their products. The leaflets mentioned children as fussy eaters who should have very carefully prepared and presented food served, for example, in the shape of a face or an animal to tempt them to eat. Science and technology were emphasised even in simple matters. Helena looked at her drawing of the milk ducts inside the breast, and when asked if she thought she might breast-feed she shuddered: 'Ugh no, it's dirty and you can't see how much the baby is getting.'

The main messages of the course appeared to be: children are very expensive and endlessly demanding; they are fussy and very hard to please; adults must never rest from guarding helpless children from all kinds of known or potential or invisible risks of infection or injury and other dangers, like patients who need nursing. There seemed to be nothing about fun, adventure, or children as actors who contribute to one another's enjoyment and learning, and no questioning of the commercial interests and pressures. Instead of encouraging students to think about consulting children, the course included many ways of discouraging them from thinking of consulting children, or thinking independently and critically themselves.

RISK AND PROBABILITY

Reasons for not consulting with young children include beliefs that they have very little idea about the future and therefore about dangers, risks and probabilities. Consulting often involves asking about past events in order to plan or alter future events. If children are too vague about past and future, they are barred from this process. Yet although the younger ones are often confused about terms like 'tomorrow', 'next week', 'in an hour' or 'soon' (perhaps because adults give this last word so many meanings) they usually have some sense of past and future.

Much depends on the way things are explained. Probability becomes clearer when children talk about how probable it might be that today: it will rain; a dragon will arrive; they will have chips for lunch; and their parents might win the lottery. Risks and associated cautions can be discussed in terms of the risks of being knocked down by a car or an elephant. Surgeons describe children aged seven or eight years as understanding the risks of major high-risk surgery in terms of the risks of crossing the road, and of painful preventive treatment of future problems in the long term as being like saving money in the bank to spend in the future (Alderson 1993).

If adults are to overcome the complications of consulting children posed by worry about risks, they need to discuss exactly which risks they are worried about and why, what benefits are lost if they do not consult children, and if there are any real risks, why they could be worth taking and how they might be shared or reduced by involving the children.

CHALLENGING CONFLICT

Other complicated matters are conflict and violence. This section considers examples of adults' influences and of how aware young children can be in responding to violence, and in preventing or resolving it. Violence is usually talked of as a problem between children. Yet adults can very much increase or reduce levels of violence in the extent to which they work respectfully with one another and with the children (Commission on Children and Violence 1995).

An account of two lunch times on a course for early years staff, who strongly reacted to the ways they were treated, shows how young children often feel. The adults enjoyed the leisurely well-planned first lunch. The second time, they became impatient, angry and uncooperative when their morning's work was suddenly interrupted, they were all hustled into the wash room together and told to hurry, but then were sat waiting for a long time at the table before the food arrived, and were told off for behaving badly (Goldschmeid and Jackson 1994). The example shows how, when staff are polite and respectful to the children, value their time and work in greater partnership and equality with them, children of all ages feel happier and behave better. So at the level of planning, policy and daily practice in early years settings, intentionally or not, the staff can powerfully incite, defuse or prevent anger and aggression. In three Save the Children early years centres which worked on anti-violence methods, it was found that the levels of violence differed in each centre. In the calmest one, with Asian staff, 'each child was treated as the centre of the universe – and with complete respect' (Finch 1998).

Research suggests that young children are highly aware of social skills and complex relationships, and like adults they use conflict skilfully to negotiate their relationships, as shown in the following two summaries of video recordings of Australian children (Danby and Barker 1998).

The jail

Amelia and Portia are four years old, Elana is three. Amelia attends the preschool centre four times a week, Elena three times and Portia only twice a week. Portia tries to lock Elana into a 'jail', the home corner, while Amelia and John watch. Elana cries and a teacher comes to find out who has upset her and 'made her sad… You have to tell me so we can solve the problem'. The teacher tells Portia to 'make her feel better' and Portia hugs Elana. The teacher thanks Portia and walks away. The four children whisper and walk around, brushing against each other. Two girls end up in the home corner, and Portia stays on her own with a teacher.

'I'm bigger'

David and John are four years old and Connell is just three. Playing with wooden blocks, the older boys say they are bigger and they will 'just BASH YOU right off… THROW you through that television' and other threats to Connell until he starts to cry very loudly. The teacher arrives and says that 'he looks very sad… Can you make him feel better please? …Give him a cuddle'. David gives a fleeting hug, but he argues with the teacher: 'We were just tricking him'. David turns his back on the teacher as she talks and, when she has gone, the boys continue to argue about who is the biggest.

The observing researchers comment that the teacher sees children's conflicts as a problem, a matter of upset feelings for teachers to resolve rather as colonial administrators tried to do, without needing to find out the details of who really did what and why. When the teacher leaves, the girls seem to continue her approach, to console and care, as if they know that a brief hug is not enough and John takes some part in this. The older boys, however, argue against and contravene the teacher's instructions, using her as a foil to show their masculine independence in contrast to her feminine concern with care for feelings.

The researchers believe that the younger children use conflict to try to increase their power by crying and calling in the teacher on to their side to blame the others. The children try to involve the watching researcher, but she does not respond so they cry louder for the teacher to hear. The scenes show how, very early on, children in a weaker position learn to turn to teachers to resolve their differences.

The teacher is seen as more concerned with pity and blame, and soothing hurt feelings to restore calm and return to 'play'. Purposeful constructive play is supposed to be the children's main occupation. Yet they seem as preoccupied with their complex relationships, as when they brush past each other to repair friendship in subtle verbal and silent cues. The researchers add that boys and girls react very differently, but it is not a simple difference; John shares in the girls' brushing past movements.

The researchers do not question where the boys' pride and anxiety about being bigger come from, and do not consider the children's motives. It is likely that Portia, who attends only twice a week, is worried that she is losing her friend Amelia to the new younger girl. She began 'jailing' Elana as if to separate her from Amelia. When children attend sessions irregularly, or less frequently than their friends, disrupted relationships can leave them feeling lonely, unsupported and even disorientated, compared with those who can warmly greet their friends when they arrive (Penn 1997a).

Teaching children to rely on adults to sort out conflict does not help them to see how they can increase or reduce or resolve conflict themselves (Holdigan 1999). This is encouraged by helping children to see themselves as effective peace-makers, instead of aggressors and victims.

BULLYING

Concerns about bullying in school are very common (Blatchford and Sharp 1994) and for thousands of children, violence from other children is an extremely serious problem. Yet frequency is sometimes confused with severity. Bullying is often reported in many schools because, rightly, adults now often enquire about it and take it seriously. To put bullying in context, the survey already mentioned of over 2,250 school students aged from seven years in the UK found that many children reported that there was some bullying in their school. However, in open questions asking what they most and least liked about their school, only 47 people cited bullying as a main concern. Whereas peers were mentioned only in the top ten likes (friends, break times), teacher featured highly in both the most-liked features (named lessons) and most-disliked features (named lessons, teachers, rules) (Alderson 1999). Contrary to most reports, the children said that their problems tended to be caused by adults rather than by other children in the school.

Some school codes go to extremes, so that 'not talking to someone', or mutually-enjoyed rough play can count as bullying and children are punished and labelled as bullies for behaviour which is not intended to harm anyone and does not actually do so (Blatchford and Sharp 1994). This can undermine the important efforts in many schools, early years centres and out-of-school clubs, mentioned earlier, to tackle bullying through involving and consulting with the children.

WORKING WITH CHILDREN TO PREVENT AND RESOLVE CONFLICT

Like the Australian video, an example from an English school teacher describes children's intense reactions to one another. She described how a newly-arrived refugee girl joined a pair of friends, and then became best friend to one of them, while the other girl became lonely, ill, very sad, and did not grow for months (Marlowe 1997).

This story was told as if it is sad but inevitable. Yet there is much that adults can do from the earliest years to encourage mixed and group friendships, so that children need rely less on exclusive best friendships and rivalries. During many activities, children can work in groups rather than pairs, and the groups can form and reform so that everyone has the chance to work and play with everyone else and get to know them well. This helps all children to feel more at ease with their whole group (McNamara and Moreton 1995). For example, they can make cards which they pick from a bowl, to see which group they will be in each time they do group work, instead of some children choosing the most popular ones and leaving the obviously least popular ones feeling left out.

A mainstream school with children aged three to eleven planned ways to protect and involve the ten per cent of profoundly-disabled children (Cleves 1999). They avoid queues and mass movements round the school, the times when conflict often occurs. They have little furniture, so reducing the chance of children knocking into things and each other and starting arguments. The children easily form and reform groups, sitting on the carpet, leaning against a work top, or quickly drawing up a few chairs. Staff try to ensure that the group are always mixed in ability, ethnicity and sex. The inclusive equal opportunities policy on ability also works well for the many children who speak English as an additional language, who are included and involved as soon as they arrive. Joint activities like making a huge collage include everyone at their own level, and help the children to enjoy each other's company. It is rare to see anyone playing alone at break times. The children are considerate almost without seeming to notice. Larger ones run around the playground and carefully miss knocking into other children.

When children are in conflict, listening to them about what is happening can provide better solutions than a quick hug. The following examples are given by Sue Finch (Finch 1998) who reviews typical adult solutions like, 'say you are sorry', giving a reward or punishment, or using time out, and she notes their limitations. Observing and talking with children can work better through watching how, when and why violence begins, making preventive plans with children, and teaching them assertive non-aggressive ways to negotiate. Puppets and masks help children to express and respond to a whole range of feelings from anger to happiness, and to act out and resolve their conflicts.

When working and playing together, people have to find a balance between feeling they have some control but also sharing and letting go. Young children generally manage this very well, but there are ways of helping them to do so, if needed. In formal group discussions, children can roll a ball or pass an object from one speaker to the next to help them to listen and take turns (Mosley 1993). If one toy is very popular, a clock or an egg-timer can time the turns, and the children can check how the time is passing (Finch 1998). There are many practical ways of preventing conflict, from the way space, time, equipment and activities are organised, to the way disputes are resolved. Competitive games like snap or musical chairs, so common that their sometime negative effects often pass unrecognised, can be avoided sometimes when they are likely to increase hostility and aggression or feelings about being better or worse than others. Children who have little free play space at home enjoy being energetic together on climbing toys and in large outdoor spaces. Early on, children enjoy cooperating in small groups, making pictures and collages together, playing music, joining in cooperative games, cooking and painting together. Children aged three years practise negotiating skills. For example, when five children wanted to play a game for only four players, the staff asked them to solve the problem. After talking about how the left-out person would feel, and about other options, the children decided to play another game (Finch 1998).

Turning arguments into questions
Some teachers encourage children to use disagreements as quest-ions to investigate. Five and six-year-olds were preparing a booklet for the new children in an Italian pre-school centre. They talked about how the children could not read and would like drawings. Someone then thought that as young children scribble they would prefer scribble drawings to more realistic ones of a map of the centre. The children prepared different drawings and then showed them to younger children to see which ones they liked best (Edwards, Gandini and Forman 1998).

PEER MEDIATION

Many schools now teach quite simple peer mediation techniques. One junior school began by inviting in experts and having a long course for the oldest children, mixed with fun and games. Younger children also tried to use the methods, and later the head teacher decided to teach them the technique herself, in short sessions. She thought these worked better without being interrupted by the games (Highfield School 1997). While I was in the school, two large eight-year-old boys came up to their class teacher and said, 'We've had a row, we need mediation.' The teacher said 'all right' and they went into the corridor with one of the youngest girls in the school. 'I don't know what they do out there', said the teacher, 'but they always come back smiling' which, in a few moments, they did.

Longer-term problems in this school are tackled in class circle times, or by the school council, which has a boy and girl member from each class. Classes may invite the parents of a child with behaviour difficulties to join their circle time, and to work out positive ways for everyone to help the child to change. The head teacher at Highfield used to spend almost all her time sorting out behaviour problems, but needed to spend a little time on them when the children took on much of the responsibility. All the staff welcome the improvements, especially the meal-time supervisors (one per 70 children) who often call on the mediators.

For mediation, the children have to agree to listen, keep calm, and not interrupt. Usually two mediators ask each person in the conflict, in turn, to tell what they think happened and why, how they feel about it, and how they think the problem could be resolved. They ask them to agree on a resolution method, and to meet in a week's time to see how it worked. The head teacher believes that some of the younger children learn mediation skills most quickly as they have fewer negative habits to unlearn. Further research in early years groups on how children can use mediation to tackle conflict is urgently needed.

POWER, CONFLICT AND VIOLENCE

Power as force or energy

In an international report on work with children, the authors keep writing about the need to change power relations between children and adults, if children are to be consulted and their ideas used with them to make improvements from individual to international levels (Johnson *et al.* 1998). Sharing power involves respecting children's views and their networks, working with them as partners as far as possible and as much as they want to. It involves changing routines and structures so that children can feel more comfortable, and included, and fairly treated. Power can be seen as (usually negative) force, or as more positive energy.

Dividing power as force

Power and rights are not generally popular words. Adults prefer to talk of their care or authority, or the need for their firm control, rather than their power over children. Child power is still less popular a term. This happens when power is seen as something to be divided rather than shared, like the slices of a cake when the more power one person has, the less everyone else has.

When adults believe they must set all the rules which the children must obey, the adults worry that if they let children have a little power they will want more and more, a process it is better not to start. This is especially so, if it is believed that children should not have any power, with fearful visions of powerless but responsible adults, and irresponsible but powerful children.

This kind of open conflict and force has been called the least powerful kind of power (Lukes 1974). People are still aware of who is setting the rules and the choices, what these are, and whether they like them, and they may resist them. A second level of power is to offer people misleading choices by not telling them all the options and information. Children might be told: 'There is only enough money to buy some small toys, not a slide you wanted,' but not be told that the staff have decided how to spend the extra available money. This could be reasonable (and the staff may be right that their choice is much better than a slide) unless they are pretending to share the full decision honestly with the children when they are not doing so.

The third and strongest kind of power as hidden force happens when people believe they have no choice and they must, and want to, behave in certain ways. Many examples of this third kind are shown by the way today's parents believe 'in their souls' that they must protect and stimulate their children, keep them very clean and provided with many commodities, in ways that would surprise parents from other centuries (Rose 1990). Again, this is often reasonable and children benefit from the newer ideas about their care. Problems arise when people are unaware of options which they would choose if they knew about them.

If adults are to consult children honestly, it is vital for them to be aware of ways in which hidden power as force can limit the methods they use for sharing ideas, and the changes which together they may want to make.

Sharing power as creative energy

Positive approaches to power see it as the essential energy which creates and channels ideas and achieves improvements. Sharing power and rights can bring greater freedom and fulfilment. One example is the young Scandinavian children mentioned earlier who enjoy being independent at home on their own, and whose parents can also then enjoy more freedom. Many small examples are given in early years centres, such as providing mattresses instead of beds so children can easily lie down when they wish, and little steps for children to climb up onto the changing table, so that they are consulted and deliberately cooperate in their care (Goldschmeid and Jackson 1994). The staff are also saved from lifting children and furniture.

Respecting children involves respecting and consulting all the staff, as this increases the chances for children also to be heard and their ideas taken seriously. The most senior person knows all the children in a busy centre and takes account of all their views in planning and policy partly by talking with them, and also by working closely with the key workers for particular children who contribute their children's ideas as well as their own. Although this is standard practice, the degrees to which junior staff are consulted and feel able to speak vary greatly.

Sharing power may involve waiting while everyone gradually works out solutions to problems and one solution perhaps leads to another, rather than a few senior people trying to act quickly. For example, the Highfield school staff and children worked for years to improve relationships and behaviour through methods like circle times, bully busters, guardian angels who flew to the rescue of children who bulled or were bullied, and peer mediation (Highfield School 1997). The goal of everyone to be positive and responsible could only be achieved through working towards that goal with them, it could not be imposed on them. A poster about mediation shows two donkeys tied together and straining in opposite directions towards two piles of hay. They cannot eat until they share the same pile (Finch 1998). Power as force means that much energy is wasted on conflict. Power as energy enables adults and children to work together toward agreed ends.

The crucial first step towards involving young children in solving problems of risk and control, conflict and violence is when adults take on more positive views of power, as creative energy which can benefit everyone when it is shared to some extent.

CHAPTER EIGHT

Working Together
Sharing Decisions and Responsibility

This chapter considers how children take responsibility for themselves and for others, and how their powerful understanding, feelings and spiritual awareness help them to share activities and decision-making with other children and with adults. Some examples are drawn from ways that children are involved in their health care and in medical decisions because the way children think, decide and act have been researched in some detail in this area. Much more detail needs to be known about how children understand, and can or want to share in making decisions, about other aspects of their lives – at home, in day care centres, at school, during leisure times, and when they need extra help, such as from social and legal services.

SHARING DECISIONS WITH OTHER CHILDREN

Can children understand democratic methods of consulting? Examples of young children listening and taking turns have already been given. Adults usually chair or facilitate the meetings, but young children could probably understand notions of the neutral chair in terms of the football referee who does not kick the ball but is there to make sure everyone else has a fair turn and keeps the rules.

The Participation Education Group in Newcastle involves people aged from about eight years upwards and has a rapidly growing membership in schools and other centres. They run Peer Induction, Education and Support (PIES) workshops for young people and adults on 19 aspects of working together. PIES cover topics like advocacy, networking, building confidence, fundraising, mediation, running events and evaluation.

Fourteen PEG members aged eight years upwards, with two adults, attended a planning meeting with researchers at London University. They wanted to work jointly on holding a two-day event in 1999 on democracy. On the train journey from Scotland and the north of England, they chose three eleven-year-old boys to chair the meeting and plan the agenda. The meeting began with everyone talking about 'why are we having this meeting?' At the end, they went round the circle, each saying what they had got out of the meeting. During the meeting, PEG members reminded the researchers of their terms which everyone present seemed to understand clearly. These standards, like avoiding jargon, respecting everyone as an expert, making sure everyone knows and agrees with the broader agenda, are also being used by children and adults with learning difficulties (Ward 1997).

PEG's principles
1. We should have an equal share of everything.
2. We should have an equal say in everything.
3. We don't want adults to talk down to us.
4. Adults who work with us should respect us.
5. Adults should use language we can follow.
6. Adults shouldn't try to take over.
7. We should be able to disagree with adults.
8. We should be able to stand up to adults.
9. We want to be able to get our opinions and ideas across to adults.
10. Children and young people should be in charge (PEG 1998).

The list echoes Arnstein's ladder of levels of participation in Chapter 5.

TAKING RESPONSIBILITY FOR YOURSELF AND OTHERS

Children can be consulted at four levels (Alderson and Montgomery 1996):

---

1. Being informed
2. Expressing a view
3. Influencing the decision-making
4. Being the main decider.

Participation is sometimes assumed to be only stage 4, leaving the child to decide, and is then dismissed as too risky. But each of the other stages are important methods of participation in their own right, and they precede the fourth stage if the child is to be able to make informed decisions. The first three levels are in the UN Convention (12, 13) which adds, 'the views of the child being given due weight in accordance with the age and maturity of the child' (12), but gives no age barrier. The first three levels include any child who can: first, understand information; or second, form a view; or third, is considered to be able to form a view which can usefully inform adults' decisions. Similarly the 1989 Children Act repeatedly advises local authorities to inform and consult with children about plans which affect them.

The UN Convention aims to bring national laws up to its own standards, but also respects national laws 'which are more conducive [than the Convention] to the realisation of the rights of the child' (41). English law goes beyond the Convention in respecting the right of children not simply to contribute to decision-making, but also to be the main decider, and to make serious personal decisions in their own right. Children can do so in law if they are able to understand the relevant information and have the discretion to make a wise choice in their best interests (Gillick v. Wisbech & W. Norfolk AHA, 1985). In English and Scottish law, this fourth-level right has no set age limit, but it does have strict competence limits; children have to convince the responsible adults that they can make an informed, sensible decision.

If this fourth level of participation is taken to mean children's rights 'to do whatever they want', 'to divorce their parents' or 'to refuse to go to school or have life-saving medical treatment' then all participation, even expressing a view or being informed, is easily dismissed as dangerous nonsense. It is believed to harm children, break up families and bring chaos into nurseries, schools and hospitals. Yet the UN Convention and English law repeatedly state that 'the best interests of the child shall be a primary consideration' (1,3,21) and the Convention makes other qualifications, as listed in Chapter 2.

At present, adults tend to have to justify consulting children about serious decisions and to demonstrate first that the child is competent. But there could be a reversed routine, in that adults would start from the premise that the child is competent to understand, and may have views, and may want to have a say. It is easier to demonstrate when a child is not competent or does not want to be involved than when they do.

EVERYDAY HEALTH CARE CHOICES

The law and research on involving young children in major personal decisions are mainly about health care. So far, young children's own views about care and contact, such as where they want to live if their parents divorce, have not yet received much research attention (O'Quigley 1999). For this reason, examples in this section on how young children can make personal decisions will be about health care. Consulting with children can avoid force and resistance and increase the informed cooperation on which their well-being depends.

> **When Susan was aged four**, diabetes was diagnosed. She knew how ill she felt when her blood sugar level was too high or low. She quickly understood and was able to explain to other people that she needed injections of insulin, which her body no longer made. She knew that insulin is 'the key that turns sugar into energy'. She learned how to do frequent blood sugar level tests, and through her diet to try to avoid levels that were too high or low. She was expert at filling the syringe with insulin correctly, flicking for bubbles, and injecting herself twice a day. Her health was in her hands as she constantly needed to show her informed commitment to her treatment and to her low protein, low sugar diet. For example, she had to refuse sweets and biscuits, and watch other children enjoying these.

Whereas some people try too hard and too long at great personal cost, others give up too soon, and unnecessarily experience loss and failure. Young children are especially liable to be pushed too hard or stopped too soon unless adults consult them and trust their judgement. This can help children's confidence to try new things, persist through difficulties, and know when to stop or try an alternative, with less fear of failure. During a research interview, Linda aged eight, who uses crutches, and a wheelchair sometimes, raised the topic of whether people should be pressured to achieve as much as possible or be given extra protection and support.

When to carry on trying

Int: Is there anything else important about your life I
          haven't asked you?

Linda: If you want to do recorder, you *try* it. Because my
          teacher says you can *do* recorder, you can *do* choir,
          you can *play* chess, you can *do* nature club.

Int: Is she saying, if you want to do something, *do* it?

Linda: Yes.

Int: Is that the way you want to live?

Linda: Yes, I'm going to learn it. Although it's quite hard
          I'm going to do it, to work hard.

Int: Is that because your teachers say 'come on, come
          on', or because you've got lots of go in you?

Linda: I've got a lot of go. [When things are hard] I don't
          give up. I try, but if it's too much I give up.

Int: That's interesting because lots of grown-ups find it
          hard to know when to try carrying on and when to
          give up.

Linda: Yes, my mummy's good about that (Alderson and
          Goodey 1998, pp.132–3).

MAJOR DECISIONS: THE EXAMPLE OF MEDICAL TREATMENT

Can and should children be consulted about major complex decisions?
Even if they can understand, do they want to take on responsibility for
them? Some of the following examples involve life-threatening illness
to show how young children can grasp ideas both intellectually and
emotionally. They suggest that young children could be consulted far
more about smaller everyday decisions. Children in a Bristol cancer
ward, even two-year-olds, understood the names of drugs and their
purpose, and cooperated with their treatment (Kendrick *et al.* 1986),
while those in an American cancer unit talked together in the toilets in
order to protect their parents from knowing how much they knew
(Bluebond-Langner 1978). A three-year-old understood that his liver
biopsy was not therapeutic but was a test and that they would 'put a little
piece of the liver under a special glass to see if it was good'. When this

example was mentioned to a four-year-old she said: 'Do you mean a microscope?' (see Krementz 1990; Cousens and Stevens 1997).

Children are not asked to make serious decisions, which involve remembering and balancing several risks and benefits, if it is assumed that they cannot think of several ideas at once. There was a brief period when pictures in children's books were expected to be very simple because children were believed to be unable to cope with 'busy' pictures. Yet young children enjoy many different and complex television programmes without confusing the separate casts and story lines.

An extreme example of complex understanding is of a seven-year-old girl talking about the risks and benefits of having a heart-lung transplant. She knew it might not work, and it might not be done in time to save her life, but she still chose to go on the transplant list (Alderson 1993, pp.162–3). She illustrates how competent young children can be. Increasingly, doctors and nurses are consulting young children about making major decisions with their parents, because they believe it is better to care for informed cooperative children who want their treatment, than for ignorant, confused and resisting children.

The young children whose views are respected often have had disrupted schooling, and have poor reading and maths skills. They are ordinary children, except in their unusually-profound experiences of illness, disability, major treatments and being near to death. They show how ability is linked to experience far more than to age or scholastic ability. A senior nurse commented: 'Their understanding of life and death knocks spots off ours.'

Fortunately, most young children are never faced with such serious and distressing decisions but those who are suggest that many young children have these capacities and courage, including some children with learning difficulties. Six of the 120 young patients in the surgery research project had identified learning difficulties and some of these had very strong preferences. One was Amy who at eight years 'was only a metre high' and was determined to go through years of very painful leg-lengthening treatment. Her mother, a physiotherapist, said that only Amy could make this kind of decision, no one could do it for her.

Most children and adults, who are able to make informed decisions, prefer others to decide with or for them. These examples are not given to suggest that young children should *have* to decide. Careful consultation can help staff and parents to find out how much children need and want to know and be involved in making decisions, and to sort out misunderstandings and unnecessary fears.

PEACE AND JUSTICE

Another way in which people take responsibility for themselves and others is through political awareness and by challenging pressures such as pollution and poverty. The annual *Blue Peter* television appeal shows young children's active concern for the environment, and for helping disadvantaged people. Can young children understand general and partly-abstract issues, such as the politics of racism, inequality and oppression? A teacher, Melissa Butler, describes how deeply conscious her class became of these issues when they discussed these intensely in class (Butler 1998):

In a class of seven-year-olds, living on a black housing estate in Chicago, Gerald once pointed his finger like a gun to Christopher's head. Ebony asked: What do you mean by that? Are you trying to kill your beautiful Black Brother? Gerald was taken aback and said *'No!'* and then looked confused.

Melissa Butler believes that knowledge is about ways of thinking and understanding, less about items to remember. The children agreed, so that if someone wanted to talk about rocks or ants or something not obviously related to justice, they would say: 'That's nice, but what does that have to do with peace and power?' 'How you gonna help your Brothers and Sisters by talking about that?' They talked about shootings, funerals, drugs, gangs and the police brutality they witnessed, to make sense of their experience and to challenge the clichés they had been taught. In this area, there are very high rates of black men in prison, and of poverty and drug-dealing. The children live with painful contradictions: gun men are cool heros yet cruel murderers; the police are said, on television, to be good, yet they kill your friends and deal out drugs and guns. Drug-dealing is bad but may be the only way to earn money for the family to live on.

Melissa Butler helped the children to think critically and logically through these contradictions, to see the immense pressures on individuals, and to move on from blaming them to working for peace and justice. Ebony shows how they became critically conscious of the 'cool' macho gun sign, which they came to call the 'gun move'. They stopped copying the older boys who used it casually and unthinkingly, and came to see how this kind of 'cool' harms their community. Yet they also kept certain 'cools' in order to survive. Adults' instructions about what they should not do contradicted the examples they observed all around them. The easy rules seven-year-olds are expected to repeat – 'I'll be good and never touch a gun or join a gang,' – cannot help them as they grow older. So they talked about social pressures and the limits of personal agency.

Awareness grew through taking everyone's stories very seriously, and appreciating layers of meaning and even inconsistencies. Consulting the children seriously involved interpreting their stories in several ways. For example, they often told stories of moving on ('Ah, uh, my mama say we be moving soon') which were stories of longing for change and release, rather than factual. They told stories about Chuckie Cheese where they enjoyed pizzas, games, family celebrations and reunions – or were telling the story as if it happened because they longed for it to happen. Respecting their stories meant seeing when stories are told in order:

- to invent what the children wished was true (a way of coping);
- to show off and impress the others (being 'cool');
- to try to fit inconsistencies into a consistent understanding of the world (making sense);
- to live with the complexities of hyper reality; or
- to develop goals and practise ideas for empowerment.

They spent the year talking about social justice, power, unity and community change, and through this developed their Brotherhood and Sisterhood, finding their place in a contradictory, unjust world, but one where they want to find hope, looking for aims to work towards instead of pressures to resist. One of the girls, Whitnesha, was expelled from her mainly-white dancing class, when the white children asked about her school: 'I just said that we learn peace and power and they just told on me. [The teacher] didn't want me telling those white kids about the projects and the other black kids. You know, Ms Butler, they is resisting me! Now what am I going to do? They need to know the truth!'

School education tends to turn practical matters into abstract ones which are harder for children to understand and become involved with, leading to assumptions that they cannot do so. But when abstract ideas about rights and justice are linked to the living reality of children's daily lives and their deep feelings, children show their knowledge and deep concern (Beane 1990; Griffiths and Davies 1995; Holden and Clough 1999). Radical ideas about theatre, developed with South American peasants (Boal 1979), are used by a team of young adults who visit English schools. The original dramas involved both actors and audience in deep experiences. For example, a woman was asked to 'sculpt' a group of people into two scenes, one when an atrocity took place in her village, the second of how she would like the villagers to be in future. All the group were then asked how they would change people from the first to the second scene, by sculpting a third scene of change. So, for example, they took away the guns or pointed them at other people, and they changed the actors' pose from begging for mercy to challenging the soldiers.

Involvement through drama

The team in England prepares the sessions by finding out pressing concerns in the school, such as bullying. Then they act a drama about it with an unhappy ending. They act the play again but stop halfway through and ask children to help them to create a happier ending. The actors will have warmed up the whole group by starting with fun and interactive sessions. They have a 'joker' as a go-between, who explains the rules, such as that everyone must use non-violent suggestions. Children as young as four years eagerly volunteer to join the drama, even in front of 200 people. They are asked to take on victim roles not aggressor ones, and young children propose and act out imaginative ways of resolving the problems in the play, helping bullies to empathise and victims to be more confident. Young children can be 'amazingly assertive' when they talk and act from their personal experiences, as if they cannot bear to stand by and watch (Helen Gregory, personal communication).

This is another example, like those detailed in Chapter 1, of how the arts bring learning alive and show children's creative and moral awareness.

These very different examples of taking responsibility for yourself and others, ranging from personal health-care choices to democratic responsibilities indicate the wide range of views and decisions on which ordinary young children can be seriously consulted.

RESPECTING VIEWS AND FEELINGS

Consulting children involves respecting their views and feelings and their ability to respect other people's feelings. Peer mediation works well at Highfield school because of changes in the school at all levels: lots of personal work on feelings and expressing them creatively in words, art and drama; guessing and describing other people's feelings; learning a rich range of words, so that hitting out is no longer the easiest way to express anger or jealousy. Equally important were structural changes in the school, the active highly-respected school council, other democratic approaches, an emphasis on practical citizenship and many enjoyable shared activities and rewards. In this school in a disadvantaged area, for example, all classes sometimes have sleep-overs at school followed by breakfast, a way of having a kind of school trip which costs nothing and encourages friendly joint activities (Highfield School 1997).

The skilful way the Italian teachers described earlier listen to the children is also shown in the way the children listen to each other. It depends on assuming that the speaker is making sense, even if at first the listener does not realise what this sense is, as shown in the next example (Gardner 1998).

Stuart, aged four, and his speech therapist look at a picture of a spotty face, to start talking about 'sp'.

Therapist: S:pots

Stuart: Bots (looking at picture).

Therapist: Pots?

Stuart: Bots (looking at therapist then away).

Therapist: Are they pots?

Stuart: (Looks to therapist again and shakes head.)

Therapist: Let's hear the Sammy snake sound at the beginning then. (Pause).h s:pot.

Stuart: Bots.

The speech therapist wants Stuart to realise his pronunciation errors and learn to correct them spontaneously. To achieve this, she tends to suggest corrections implicitly and does not tell Stuart exactly what she wants him to do and why, as if she thinks that if Stuart becomes conscious of the problem and the correction he will not be able to do this spontaneously, and almost subconsciously. The main topic of her conversation is sounds, but Stuart assumes that, as in ordinary conversation, the main issue is the sense and meaning of the words not their sounds, and the aim is to check whether the things in the picture actually are spots. It is not that Stuart is too limited to understand the therapist's rules, but that she does not explain them. Stuart is skilful in the ordinary rules of conversation and keeps trying to apply them here but his efforts are not seen by the therapist as sense (trying to follow the usual rules), but as non-sense (not following any rules) and as a failure to understand sounds and 'repair errors'.

It could be helpful for the therapist to treat Stuart more as an informed partner. She could look at why Stuart's responses make sense to him, and explain to him her agenda. Before being able to correct himself spontaneously, Stuart has to understand her aim of teaching him a new skill (pronouncing 'sp'), and how and when to use it. This would involve moving from a rather behaviourist-training approach to an explicitly discussed and shared agenda, spending more time on consulting and appealing to his informed cooperation, and less on instruction.

COMMUNICATING BEYOND WORDS

Another way of respecting the youngest children's views and feelings is to move beyond words. Valuable ways of consulting and learning from babies and children beyond words have been developed, for example, by psychotherapy. This gives insights into children's profound understanding of their difficulties and needs, as the account of Dib's play shows (Axline 1966). One young boy painted a flower with nine petals nine days before he died of cancer (Kubler Ross 1983). When many such examples are given together they seem to have more than chance meanings. Even sceptics may still be puzzled by the striking differences between drawings like Figure 8.1 and the usual ones by six-year-olds and wonder what the child does understand and believe.

A child may be too young or too sick to share verbally in making health-care decisions, yet may influence decisions through expressed feelings and body language. Samantha aged six wanted to have her first two liver transplants, and showed she understood what was involved when she explained them to her class at school. When these failed she became very distressed and resisting, so much so that her parents sadly decided that they would refuse the third attempt, with its very small hope of success, for her sake not for their own real preference. After she died, her mother felt they had been right in respecting her wish (Irwin 1996). It is sometimes assumed that words are the only genuine way to communicate, body language is mistrusted as vague and misleading. Yet words too can be misleading or confusing. Bodies can be the source of profound knowledge, when children learn through their illness and disability, and express themselves physically.

Figure 8.1 The six suns

A boy, aged six, with a life-threatening illness, who was not willing to talk about it, drew a slide which came to a dramatic stop in mid-air.
The boy's therapist said that when they talked about the drawing:

> I felt that he seemed to convey here the feeling that he was on a
> fast-moving downward course, which suddenly stops, possibly

leading to a feeling of falling (if we notice that the bottom of the slide is well above ground level.) Again, this confirms that the abrupt ending was ahead of him.

The sun in a picture often denotes the parental presence, or, in drawings of bereaved children, it is often placed over the dying or dead family member. The ordinary or usual depiction of the sun in a six-year-old's picture would be in a corner. This unusual display of suns here seems to carry a rich range of meanings: the six suns refer to his six years, which stop at the point where the slide stops; they hang over the picture oppressively, conveying both an over-attentive parent as well as, possibly, marking out the *whole* slide: he was leaving no doubt that this symbol of the person who is dying truly 'covers' the area. Interestingly, this child had never really thrived: he had experienced severe eating difficulties all his life. This background seems to tie in with the oppressive suns, which go back to the 'beginning', in the past – the left of the picture.

This drawing opened up the possibility of talking about his fears, and, indeed, his awareness that he was dying, but my comments on the picture are not meant to be prescriptions or recipes for interpreting other drawings: any understanding of a drawing is arrived at in conjunction with the child's comments, the situation in which the drawing is made, and possibly the overall knowledge of the child. Wide experience of the normal developmental stages through which children's drawings evolve is also important, as a yardstick for any unusual or striking features (Judd 1995, p.35).

Consulting children by asking them to draw can gain illuminating evidence (Bach 1969), but many drawings are ambiguous or vague sketches, and it is better to use them together with spoken or written comments from the child, explaining the picture. A smiling face to the viewer might have been a sad face to the artist.

Arguments against consulting children refer to their lack of moral sense. Yet when talking with children, some philosophers have noted their empathy, sharing, turn-taking and reciprocation, and their ability from their second year to begin to talk about distributive justice, fairness based on merit, goodness, equality, and benefiting the disadvantaged, questions which still perplex philosophers (Damon 1988). There appears to be greater formal moral understanding in terms of right and wrong in three-year-olds than in two-year-olds, and a firmer sense of obligation to others though, as with adults, this competes with self-interest. Pritchard (1991, 1996) believes that children enter school with well-developed moral understanding and dispositions, which schools can expand through reasoned debate, rather than simply by trying to instruct children about differences between right and wrong. He describes his complex discussions with six to seven-year-olds about lying, fair punishment, or why the choice of three children to watch a television programme should count for more than one child's choice. Videos and detailed analysis of six-year-olds' discussions also show how skilfully they anticipate and prevent conflict when, for example, they work in pairs building a Lego model (Saunders and Freeman 1998).

SPIRITUALITY

Ways of consulting young children can include appealing to their spiritual wisdom. Spiritual awareness has been described as knowing there is: 'something more than meets the eye, something more than the material, something more than the obvious, something to wonder at, something to respond to' (Copley, quoted in Stone 1995). Young children tend to be very ready to wonder and admire, and to respond with fascination to simple things like snails inching along. All aspects of life can evoke wonder; maths, for example, concerns mysteries like space, time and infinity. Consulting and learning from children includes sharing their silences and absorbed attentiveness.

Spiritual awareness involves living intensely in the present, a capacity which people tend to lose as they get older. Being absorbed in the present can deepen feelings of delight or distress, and also make them seem to last much longer, which brings advantages and disadvantages. There are ways of helping children to be more conscious of their inner life and a little less vulnerable to distressing feelings. The methods involve learning consciously to be relaxed yet alert, and to enjoy experiences through the senses and imagination. Breathing slowly, people can experience a kind of mild hypnosis which taps 'the creative, therapeutic and spiritual potentialities of the imagination' (Raban 1987). Guided imagery can be used to deal positively with feelings, such as fear or dislike, anger, destructiveness or rejection. It can help to increase respect for oneself, other people, living things, and objects. A meditation might ask children to imagine being a leaf through from bud to leaf mould, or to imagine being someone who is rejected and then accepted as in the ugly duckling story.

Another value in guided imagery is the profound insights that can emerge from subconscious knowledge. Adults who attend a visualisation session followed by drawing, painting and talking about the images are often surprised to gain new understanding of their memories and hopes, and links between them. Young children too may create poems or paintings, and talk in pairs or groups, after a visualisation. Like brainstorming, it can be a way of tapping highly-imaginative ideas which might seem impractical at first until perhaps a way is found to use them, such as in planning a garden or playground, or solving a problem.

As with all contact with young children, there are the dangers of adults misusing their power in brain-washing or social engineering. Yet the power and depths of young children's imagination and spiritual awareness can lead to enriching and rewarding sessions for them and the adults who share experiences with them.

CHILDREN COPING WITH DISTRESS, FEAR AND PAIN

Young children who feel distress can become adept at controlling their feelings. Adults who teach them to do this are, in a sense, consulting and appealing to their inner resources of self-control. Methods like blowing bubbles or bird whistles help to distract and relax children through deeper breathing. Nurses consult very young children about their levels of pain. For instance, a girl might be asked to point at the position she feels she is at on a row of faces from laughing to crying. Or a boy is asked to point at a number from one to ten to show how bad his pain feels. Nurses also help children to use high technology equipment, personal analgesia control pumps to regulate their levels of pain relief medication between previously set upper and lower limits (Llewellyn 1993).

Guided imagery is used in some hospitals to help children to create their own happy secret place in their imagination (Madders 1987), if they feel distressed. Five-year-olds can learn to use this by themselves after a few sessions. Each story has a beginning, middle and end. Before it begins, the child sits or lies as comfortably as possible and breathes slowly, eyes closed. The same kind of story can be used with groups of children. One way is to agree on the kind of place first, and perhaps to look at pictures of, for example, the sea side. Another is to tell a very general story, so that each child can imagine a different place: What colours can you see? What sounds can you hear? What can you feel with your hands? And your feet?

Guided imagery

Imagine you are going down ten steps very slowly, counting as you go down. At the bottom there is a door. What colour is it? Open the door slowly, and what do you see? (Some children see a wood, a room, a spaceship, a hot air balloon, or a beach.) Hear the sound of the waves gently breaking on the sand and the shingle stones rolling with the waves. Feel the warm sand between your toes. Walk over the wet sand to the edge of the waves and see the blue and green and white water. Feel it creeping over your feet and walk into the waves. As they come rushing up towards you, feel them gently lift you over the edge of the wave. Now you are safely swimming and floating in the warm water which gently lifts and carries you. Some fish swim round you in a dance. Some pink and green seaweed floats past spreading out its pattern in the water. Now the sea carries you back to the sand. You feel fresh and cool in the warm sunshine. You are so tired you lie down on the sand to rest and to listen to the waves and the other children playing. Now it is time to go back to the door, through the doorway, close the door behind you. Now walk up the steps, count them as you go and at the top you will back here again.

Young children's use of guided imagery shows the power of their imaginations and their courage when coping with serious illness and distress.

PERSONAL AND GENERAL PRESSURES

This book has concentrated on individuals and small groups, in trying to convey how ordinary young children live every day in sophisticated and varied ways. Yet general pressures on children and adults greatly affect their daily living together, and it would be misleading to ignore these large-scale influences. Although many British families are prosperous, there are growing constraints on children. There is the slide into poverty which now traps one in three British children (Wilkinson 1994; Qvortrup *et. al.* 1994; DSS 1995; Hutton 1995). There is concern that growing numbers of children are involved in crime, and that welfare states are shrinking; parenting is being privatised with parents being held much more responsible for their children socially and economically (O'Neill 1994). This moves away from older ideas of extended families, close communities and friendly neighbours.

To ignore these influences would imply that everyone has entirely free will to make moral choices, as liberal journalists in the UK media tend to do. Yet some people are far more free to make moral choices than others. The difference between having a garden or safe pleasant area where children can play together fairly independently, and living in bed and breakfast accommodation with stressed neighbours whose only communication is to complain about noise, radically affects family dynamics.

It is often argued that if some people cope well with such difficulties it denigrates them, and wrongly excuses those who do not cope, to plead that social pressures limit moral choice. This reverses sense and logic. The argument naively assumes that everyone is equally strong or weak, whereas everyone is to some degree unique, in both their attributes and circumstances, including children in the same family. It would be more logical to appreciate children who manage to surmount serious difficulties, and to investigate how they do so, than to regard such survival as some kind of norm which everyone can and should equally easily achieve.

Another pressing question is how best adults can treat young children as trusted, responsible people when they lie, cheat, bully, disrupt and destroy. And people working with disadvantaged children, who are distressed through the effects of poverty, illness, war, neglect or abuse, may be thinking that the examples of trusted, responsible children must belong to privileged groups. This is why examples through the book have included disadvantaged and difficult children. Frequently, the children who are most energetically disruptive become leaders in, for example, helping to raise standards of behaviour in school (Highfield School 1997) or welcoming and supporting disabled children (Cleves 1999). It is as if babies are not born as good or bad people, but as pre-moral people with more or less energy and independence. Their strengths are channelled into positive or negative ways, partly through their own choices and partly through their experiences and adults' powerful expectations.

Some readers will be concerned that encouraging children to be responsible and respecting their rights undermines the authority of strictly controlling parents, and creates disharmony and unhappiness in these families. How to complement and support parents' care, often in groups of children from widely different backgrounds, is a constant question for people working with young children. Examples in Britain (Whalley 1992; Save the Children 1995, 1997b; Cleves 1999; Kiddle 1999) or in Italy (Edwards, Gandini and Forman 1998) show the importance of working together respectfully with parents and other members of the children's families as well as with the children.

CHAPTER NINE

The Key Messages from the Evidence and Experience

The examples through this book give a few from countless, mainly unrecorded, instances of young children's capacities to relate and understand as reasonable people. Many are willing and able to be responsible, to share in caring for themselves and for others, and in making decisions with other children and with adults. The six-month-old baby who wants to share her biscuit with her family shows these early impulses.

RIGHTS AND OBLIGATIONS

The UN Convention on the Rights of the Child 1989 is reviewed in Chapter 1 as a practical and principled framework for involving children. Their participation rights complement and overlap with their protection and provision rights. To sense and respond to babies' views and feelings, as parents and carers find, establishes habits of informed co-operation. These habits are more beneficial and educational than adults simply instructing and organising – and potentially working against – children and teenagers. The Convention transforms what were formerly defined as welfare, needs and interests, dependent on adults' definitions and good will, on whim or privilege, into equal entitlements for all children and shared obligations. Children's rights to express their views on matters which affect them enable them to take a responsible share in defining their rights and obligations.

CHILDREN AS PEOPLE

Children have more in common with adults than differences from them. Children actively learn through relationships with adults and other children, through their feelings and bodies, through sharing activities and ideas, especially in small groups and away from strong relationships of authority and dependence. Education which is over-dominated by notions of active adults teaching relatively passive children under-uses children's powerful learning capacities. Policy, practice and research which appreciate children as social beings in their daily context, and go beyond the strong traditions of seeing them as isolated individuals, reveal children as much more competent than was formerly thought possible.

Changes in thinking and expression vary throughout life, especially in the early years, but these are perhaps better understood as changes of degree, rather then of kind. People come to think in more complicated ways, but not in entirely different ways. By five years, children have the kinds of intelligence, such as about self and others, language, physics, technology and the arts, which last a life time.

COMPETENCE AND INTELLIGENCE

Children's strengths are often seen more clearly during adversity, when they cope well with deprivations and difficulties. These children, who are ordinary in all but their exceptional experiences, are often below average at school. They may be refugees or severely disabled, have been looked after by a local authority, or have endured racism. They challenge assumptions that children's competence relates to their measured intelligence, reading and maths ability, and placid compliance. Children who are fortunate to live sheltered and even privileged lives may be misperceived as inevitably very dependent when they do not have the chance to show their potential strengths. A further mistake is to assume that disadvantaged children are even less competent than sheltered ones. Competence grows through experience rather than with age or ability and very young children can have profound understanding.

GENDER AND AGE

Very early in life, children adopt gender roles, learning how to be a little boy or a little girl in numerous subtle ways endorsed by their society. Many adults become concerned when masculinity is over-identified with, for example, being strong and femininity with being weak. The same process happens with age. Children obviously benefit from having strong, wise, stable adults to care for them but, as with gender, there are disadvantages in over-identifying strengths with one group and weaknesses with the opposite group. Adults can become over-confident in their own abilities and unaware of their weakness. Children, as women once were, can be forced into a false helplessness and vulnerability, and be punished if they resist. Children are often trapped in a double bind, whether they comply and are seen as good but dependent and therefore not responsible, or they try to be more independent but are seen as naughty and therefore irresponsible. The growing awareness of sexism and racism in the early years needs also to be applied to ageist prejudices and the over-infantilising of children.

THEORIES OF CHILDHOOD

Adults' and children's beliefs about young children's competence shape behaviour and are self-fulfilling. People often confuse *inherent* biological dependence with *structural* social dependence, much of which is imposed by attitudes and ways of living (Lansdown 1995). To increase respect for children's views and feelings involves shifting public and professional thinking towards more realistic appreciation of young children's abilities, so that adults engage with children's reasoning, rather than trying to control them through coercion and fear (Astington 1993).

One way forward is for adults to observe a baby in a group carefully for ten minutes. This is not a matter of getting rid of theories and seeing the 'real child'. Thinking always involves theories, in the sense of beliefs about what it means to be a child or an adult, and what kinds of behaviour are acceptable or not, and these shape how children live in different societies. But testing theories in real settings is the first step towards moving on from the theories about inexorable, slow, child development that have dominated this century, towards more realistic theories that fit more nearly with how varied, versatile, competent and intensely aware children are. The play worker who was very surprised that young children could express clear views and do research (Introduction) shows this rewarding process.

TIME AND SPACE

Children's time and space are increasingly organised by adults, in homes, nurseries, playgroups and schools, public streets and leisure spaces. Over the past century, children have become more institutionalised away from public places they once shared with adults, and are the most closely surveyed, measured and regulated age group. They are safer and perhaps happier but many are much lonelier and there is less scope for children and the adults working with them to make spontaneous choices. To think about children's daily lives and welfare, starting from their viewpoints and rights, illuminates when their care is organised for adults' convenience, and against children's best interests. 'Safety' arguments are used to constrict children's daily lives.

CONSULTING YOUNG CHILDREN

When adults routinely listen to children and consult and reflect with them, they help to increase children's competencies, and mutual trust and confidence. 'Giving children a voice' is a popular slogan, but children have voices, it is adults who need to listen. Anyone hoping to benefit people of any age tend to do so far more effectively by involving them as partners in their plans as far as possible. Practical methods of working with babies and young children have been described through the book.

BARRIERS TO WORKING WITH CHILDREN

Yet the major barrier to consulting is not children's (in)abilities, or adults' lack of skill, but prejudices that young children cannot or should not be consulted. For this reason, beliefs about childhood and about consulting children are main topics in this report, since examples of responsive children from observations or meticulous research are not going to convince people who deeply believe in older ideas about children's incapacities. The pros and cons of consulting children, set out in Chapter 3, according to what is right or beneficial or educational, are offered to encourage adults to discuss their beliefs and their deeper feelings about involving children. These beliefs and feelings can work as conduits or as barriers, like blocked pipes.

Concerns about risk and control, conflict and violence are important barriers which need to be addressed at many levels: from local communities giving more support to adults who take reasonable risks in respecting children's choices, such as going on outings, or playing outside more freely; to school education for future carers and parents about young children; to the government involving young children in forming policies, as it has promised to do in ratifying the UN Convention; and to the mass media being much more respectful towards children.

The ideas in this book are offered for adults to discuss and adapt because consulting children involves flexibly working with them rather than applying pre-set plans. Consultations and research are more likely to work well, and be taken as evidence of young children's great capacities, if all the adults concerned are committed and expect the consultations to work well.

Arguments about research methods, including sometimes well-founded criticisms, may mask deeper disagreements and fears about betraying adults, and children, and morality generally, if research findings about competent children are taken seriously.

PRACTICAL INTERACTIONS

Consultation tends to be seen in mental terms, as talking, thinking and choosing. Very young children might seem to have little part in this before they can talk confidently and fluently. Yet they can be involved, when consulting is also seen as sharing activities and feelings, and when each stage and method of researching or consulting with children is planned and designed as much as possible with their help. Then adult expertise changes from knowing what is best for them, to working skilfully with children instead of simply for them.

RESEARCH METHODS

Quantitative surveys provide valuable evidence, so too do the intensive studies which can only be done with a few children. It is important to use appropriate methods, rather than seeing certain methods as better or inferior. Whereas large numbers are necessary, for example, to measure levels of provision or poverty and to make generalisations, very few children need be involved to describe their daily life or to disprove a generalisation. A few three-year-olds, for instance, can show that *some* of them are able to do things which experts used to believe could only be achieved by older children. They may be exceptional children, it does not matter as long as researchers do not over-generalise from any type of research.

Most published examples are about children and adults working together individually or in small groups. The studies contain a wealth of information to inform parents and professionals, and local, national and international policies. Some of the examples could be drawn together into broader reports covering local, national and international examples to complement and reinforce one another. Such overviews help to clarify how the research is political as well as personal, with implications for many children on how they are consulted or excluded from sharing in decisions about resources.

WORK AND PLAY

The project on dinosaurs by five and six-year-olds, in Chapter 6, raises questions about how work and play overlap, when they are different, who works and who plays. There are advantages and disadvantages in combining play and playful methods with working with young children. It is important to be clear about what kinds of play are used, why, and how they might clarify or confuse communication.

POWER

Working with children more equally involves sharing power with them. This further involves rethinking negative beliefs about 'power' as positive energy, and transforming negative views of 'children's rights'. Rights are equal entitlements for all members of the human family, to respect their worth and dignity, as the 'foundation of freedom, peace and justice in the world' in present and future generating, as stated in the UN 1989 Convention.

MUTUAL TRUST

Young children can show their maturity when adults are mature and confident. Shared trust partly depends on people of all ages searching for the meaning in each others' words and actions, even if these at first seem non-sense. The non-sense may occur when young children, far from not following any rules, are following complex rules which adults do not at first recognise, as shown in the example of speech therapy in Chapter 8. Young children's grasp of rules is shown, for example, by how they can quickly learn thousands of words and also the grammar which holds words together.

When interviewed during research about children's wisdom to make major decisions about surgery, a hospital chaplain and former headmaster spoke of adults being 'big enough to surrender power', and to trust children who wish to make the most serious of all decisions. He asked:

But are you going to lay on children the weight of their future? Perhaps let them make a decision that could lead to their death? These are impossible questions, but hospital staff have to find the answers. Am I big enough to say: 'Whatever you choose will be valued, even if you decide against the tide; okay, you've made that decision, I'll do all I can to support you, and we'll go forward together'? It's such a big step for the adult to surrender power to the child (Alderson 1993, p.143).

SCIENTIFIC MODESTY

Over three centuries, manuals about the care of young children show startling swings of fashion between indulgence and Spartan strictness. Judy Dunn (1977, p.115) advises caution.

As parents, we have to hope that we know what we are doing with our children: to trust our eyes and feelings. As scientists, we have to recognise how little we can as yet know anything of the sort, and we have a duty not to pretend to know any more that we do in fact know. Scientific modesty is not a virtue, it is an obligation. And when what we are speaking of is what from the beginning makes for human joy and human pain this is an obligation we should take seriously.

One safeguard against extremes is to try to listen to children and to work out with them ways of living together which are rewarding for children and adults.

THE TWENTY-FIRST CENTURY

The twentieth century saw huge changes in relationships between men and women in many countries. Women are no longer routinely infantilised but are seen as adult equals to men. The changes have challenged men's power and convenience, and have brought many problems for men and women and for family life. Yet the advantages of greater justice, respect, care and equality between men and women, and more rewarding relationships, are usually believed to outweigh the disadvantages of the changed status of women.

Similarly, the twenty-first century may bring great changes for children, through more respect for their undoubted abilities, so that they are no longer misguidedly 'infantilised' – treated as far less able than they actually are. 'Infant' literally means without a voice, but as this book has shown, even babies have voices and sensible views. With greater respect for children, there will be greater justice, care that is more deeply informed by children's views and interests, and awareness of the major contributions children make. Adults who treat babies and children as sensitive, thoughtful people have very rewarding relationships with them.

Although this book has not attempted to cover global aspects of children's rights, it is set in the context of a world with much injustice, poverty and war. The average age of people in the world is 22 years so that most people are children and teenagers. The only hope for peace, justice and prosperity in the global village is the massive transfer of power and resources from white to black peoples, from men to women, and from aging minority societies to the much younger majority world – 83 per cent of the world's population. This cannot happen until rich adults trust poor young people. Prejudices are too deeply entrenched for the World Bank and other policy leaders to change their attitudes to young people unaided. A crucial task for all societies early in the twenty-first century, if there is to be any hope in solving the world's main problems, is to rethink traditions which denigrate children, so that adults can learn from and with children how to create a better future.

References

Abbott, L. and Moylett, H. (eds) (1997) *Working with the Under-threes: Responding to Children's Needs*. Buckingham: Open University Press.

Advisory Centre for Education (ACE) (1995) *Children's Voices in Schools Matters: Report of an ACE Survey into School Democracy*. London: ACE.

Alderson, P. (1993) *Children's Consent to Surgery*. Buckingham: Open University Press.

Alderson, P. (1995) *Listening to Children: Ethics and Social Research*. Barkingside: Barnardo's.

Alderson, P. (1998) Theories in health care and research. *British Medical Journal 317*, 1007–10.

Alderson, P. (1999) *Civil Rights in School: Research Briefing*. Swindon: Economic and Social Research Council.

Alderson, P. and Montgomery, M. (1996) *Health Care Choices: Making Decisions with Children*. London: Institute for Public Policy Research.

Alderson, P. and Goodey, C. (1998) *Enabling Education: Experiences in Special and Ordinary Schools*. London: Tufnell Press.

Aries, P. (1962) *Centuries of Childhood*. Harmondsworth: Penguin.

Arnstein, S. (1969) A ladder of citizen participation. *Journal of the American Institute of Planners 35*, 4, 216–24.

Astington, J. (1993) *The Child's Discovery of the Mind*. Cambridge MA: Harvard University Press.

Audit Commission/HMI (1992) *Getting in on the Act*. London: HMSO.

Audit Commission (1994) *Seen But Not Heard: Coordinating Child Health and Social Services for Children in Need*. London: HMSO.

Axline, V. (1966) *Dibs in Search of Self*. London: Gollancz.

Bach, S. (1969) *Spontaneous Paintings of Severely Ill Patients: A Contribution to Psychosomatic Medicine*. Basle: Geigy, J. R.

Barrett, H. (1998) Protest-despair-detachment: Questioning the myth. In I. Hutchby and and J. Moran Ellis (eds) *Children and Social Competence: Arenas of Action*. London: Falmer, pp.64–84.

Bawden, A., Abdullah, J., Scott, C., Lovell, C., Lally, M. and Bateren, G. (1997) *Child Care and Regeneration: Meeting the Needs of Parents and Children*. London: Save the Children.

Beane, J. (1990) *Affect in the Curriculum: Towards Democracy, Dignity and Diversity.* New York: Teacher's College Press.

Beardsley, L. (1990) *Good Day Bad Day: The Child's Experience of Childcare.* New York: Teacher's College Press.

Beck, U. (1997) Democratisation of the family. *Childhood 4*, 2, 151–68.

Becker, S. and Aldridge, J. (1995) Children who care. In B. Franklin (ed) *The Handbook of Children's Rights.* London: Routledge.

Bemak, F. (1996) Street researchers: A new paradigm redefining future research with street children. *Childhood 3*, 2, 147–56.

Black, M. (ed) (1991) *The Convention: Child Rights and UNICEF Experienced at the Country Level.* Florence: UNICEF.

Blake, W. (1958) Songs of innocence, and Songs of experience. In J. Bronowski (ed) *William Blake.* First published 1789 and 1794. Harmondsworth: Penguin.

Blatchford, P. (1998) *Social Life in School: The Role of Break Time.* London: Institute of Education.

Blatchford, P. and Sharp, S. (1994) *Break-Time and the School: Understanding and Changing Playground Behaviour.* London: Kegan Paul.

Bluebond-Langner, M. (1978) *The Private Worlds of Dying Children.* Princeton NJ: Princeton University Press.

Boal, A. (1979) *Theatre of the Oppressed.* London: Pluto.

Boyden, J. and Ennew, J. (1997) *Children in Focus: A Manual for Participatory Research with Children.* Stockholm: Rädda Barnen.

Bradley, B. (1989) *Visions of Infancy.* Cambridge: Polity Press.

Bråten, S. (1996) When toddlers provide care: Infants' companion space. *Childhood 3*, 449–65.

British Association for Child Health (1995) *Child Health Rights: A Practitioner's Guide.* London: BACCH/CRDU/RCN/ICHG.

Brown, B. (1998) *Unlearning Discrimination in the Early Years.* Stoke-on-Trent: Trentham Books.

Brown, B. (1989) Anti-racist practice is good practice. In V. Williams (ed) (1989) *Babies in Daycare: An Examination of the Issues.* London: The Daycare Trust pp.39–43.

Bruner, J. (1966) *Towards a Theory of Instruction.* New York: W W Norton.

Bruner, J. (1980) *Under Five in Britain.* London: Grant McIntyre.

Burman, E. (1994) *Deconstructing Developmental Psychology.* London: Routledge.

Butler, M. (1998) Negotiating place: The importance of children's realities. In S. Steinberg and J. Kincheloe (eds) *Students as Researchers: Creating Classrooms that Matter.* London: Falmer pp.94–112.

Cavet, J. (1998) *People Don't Understand: Children, Young People and their Families Living with a Hidden Disability.* London: National Children's Bureau.

Children's Rights Office/AMA (1995a) *Checklist for Children: Local Authorities and the UN Convention on the Rights of the Child.* London: AMA Press Section.

Children's Rights Office (1995b) *Building Small Democracies, the Implications of the UN Convention on the Rights of the Child for Respecting Children's Civil Rights within the Family.* London: Children's Rights Office.

Children's Society (1998) *No Lessons Learnt.* London: Children's Society.

Christensen, P. and James, A. (2000) *Research with Children: Perspectives and Practices.* London: Falmer/Routledge.

Commission for Racial Equality. (1996) *Exclusion from School: The Public Cost.* London: Commission for Racial Equality.

Cleves School (1999) P. Alderson (ed) *Learning and Inclusion: The Cleves School Experience.* London: David Fulton.

Commission for Racial Equality – CRE (1996) *From Cradle to School: A Practical Guide to Race Equality and Child Care.* Second edition. London: Commission for Racial Equality.

Commission on Children and Violence (1995) *Children and Violence.* London: Calouste Gulbenkian Foundation.

Cousens, P. and Stevens, M. (1997) The rights of the child in a paediatric oncology unit. In M. John. (ed) *A Charge Against Society: The Child's Right to Protection.* London: Jessica Kingsley Publishers.

Cox, M. (1997) *Children and the Arts: Creative Action for the Next Millenium.* Birmingham: Playtrain.

Cullingford, C. (1992) *Children and Society: Children's Attitudes to Politics and Power.* London: Cassell.

Cumber, C. (1989) A community nursery in action. In V. Williams (ed) (1989) *Babies in Daycare: An Examination of the Issues.* London: The Daycare Trust pp.23–7.

Cunliffe, E. and English, C. (1997) *The First Report of Kids Count: A Children's Rights Project.* Newcastle: Royal Victoria Infirmary.

Curtis, A. (1996) Do we train our early childhood educators to respect children? In C. Nutbrown (ed) (1996a) *Respectful Educators – Capable Learners: Children's Rights in Early Education.* London: Paul Chapman.

Dahlberg, G., Moss, P. and Pence, P. (1999) *Beyond Quality in Early Childhood Services.* London: Falmer Press.

Damon, W. (1988) *The Moral Child.* New York: Free Press.

Danby, S. and Barker, C. (1998) What's the problem? Restoring order in the preschool classroom. In I. Hutchby and J. Moran Ellis (eds) (1998) *Children and Social Competence: Arenas of Action.* London: Falmer.

David, T. (1992) 'Do we have to do this?' The Children Act 1989 and obtaining children's view in early childhood settings. *Children & Society 6,* 3, 204–11.

David, T. (1996) Their right to play. In C. Nutbrown (ed) (1996a) *Respectful Educators – Capable Learners: Children's Rights in Early Education.* London: Paul Chapman.

Daycare Trust (n.d.) *Listening to Children: Young Children's Views on Childcare, a Guide for Parents.* London: Daycare Trust.

Department for Education and Employment (DfEE). (1998a) *Early Years Development and Child Care: Partnership, Planning, Guidance, 1999–2000*. London: Stationery Office.

Department for Education and Employment. (1998b) *School Standards and Framework Act*. London: Stationery Office.

Department for Social Security (1995) *Households Below Average Income (HBA1): A Statistical Analysis (1979–1992/93)*. London: Stationery Office.

Department of Health. (1989) *Children Act*. London: Stationery Office.

Doise, W. and Myng, L. (1981) *La Construction Sociale de l'Intelligence*. Paris: Intereditions.

Donaldson, M. (1978) *Children's Minds*. Glasgow: Fontana.

Duffy, B. (1998) *Supporting Creativity and Imagination in the Early Years*. Buckingham: Open University Press.

Dunn, J. (1977) *Distress and Comfort*. Glasgow: Fontana.

Dunn, J. (1993) *Young Children's Close Relationships: Beyond Attachment*. London: SAGE.

Dunn, J. (ed) (1995) Connections between emotion and understanding in development. *Cognition and Emotion 9*, 2–3, 113–285.

EACH – European Association for Children in Hospital (1993) *Charter for Children in Hospital*. In *Bulletin of Medical Ethics 92*, 13–15.

Early Childhood Education Forum. (1998) *Quality and Diversity in Early Learning*. London: National Children's Bureau.

Economic and Social Research Council. (1996) *Brochure of the Research Programme, Children 5–16*, 1996–1999.

Edwards, C., Gandini, I. and Forman, G. (1998) *The Hundred Languages of Children*. London: Ablex.

Eisenberg, N. (1992) *The Caring Child*. Hove: Erlbaum Associates.

Elfer, P. and Selleck, D. (In press) *The Best of Both Worlds: Enhancing the Experience of Young Children in the Nursery*. London: National Children's Bureau.

Ennew, J. (1997) *Monitoring Children's Rights: Indicators for Children's Rights Project*. Newmarket: Global Gutter Press.

Ennew, J. and Connolly, M. (1996) Introduction: Children out of Place. *Childhood 3*, 2, 131–46.

Ensing, J. (1996) Inspection of early years in schools. In C. Nutbrown (ed) (1996a) *Respectful Educators – Capable Learners: Children's Rights in Early Education*. London: Paul Chapman.

European Commission Network on Childcare (1996) *Quality Targets in Services for Young Children*. Brussels: EC Network on Children.

Faulkner, J. (1998) Participatory video-making in Brazil. In V. Johnson, E. Ivan-Smith, G. Gordon, P. Pridmore and P. Scott (eds) *Stepping Forward: Children's and Young People's Participation in the Development Process*. London: Intermediate Technology Publications, pp.88–91.

Finch, S. (1998) *'An Eye for an Eye Leaves Everyone Blind': Teaching Young Children to Settle Conflicts without Violence.* London: National Early Years Network: Save the Children.

Fisher, J. (1996) *Starting from the Child? Teaching and Learning from 4 to 8.* Buckingham: Open University Press.

Franklin, B. (1995) *A Handbook of Children's Rights.* London: Routledge.

Frönes, I. (1994) Dimensions of childhood. In J. Qvortrup, M. Bardy, G. Sgritta and H. Wintersberger (eds) (1994) *Childhood Matters: Social Theory, Practice and Politics.* Aldershot: Avebury.

Gardner, H. (1993) *The Unschooled Mind: How Children Think and How Schools Should Teach.* London: Fontana.

Gardner, H. (1998) Social and cognitive competencies in learning: Which is which? In I. Hutchby and J. Moran-Ellis (eds) (1998) *Children and Social Competence: Arenas of Action.* London: Falmer. pp.115–33.

Gardner, R. (1989) *Who says? Choice and Control in Care.* London: National Children's Bureau.

Giller, H. and Tisdall, K. (1997) Children's services plans: Opportunities for early years workers? *Co-ordinate 60,* 6–8.

Gillick v Wisbech & W. Norfolk AHA, [1985], 3All ER. For a review of complications following this Law Lord's ruling see P. Alderson and J. Montgomery (1996) *Health Care Choices: Making Decisions with Children.* London: Institute for Public Policy Research.

Goldschmeid, E. (1989) Play and learning in the first year of life. In V. Williams (ed) 1989 *Babies in Daycare: An Examination of the Issues.* London: The Daycare Trust pp.7–17.

Goldschmeid, E. and Jackson, S. (1994) *People Under Three: Young Children in Day Care.* London: Routledge.

Goldschmeid, S. and Selleck, D. (1996) *Communication between Babies in their First Year, Video and Pack.* London: National Children's Bureau.

Green, J. (1997) *Risk and Misfortune: The Social Construction of Accidents.* London: University College London Press.

Griffiths, R. (1998) *Educational Citizenship and Independent Learning.* London: Jessica Kingsley Publishers.

Griffiths, M. and Davies, L. (1995) *In Fairness to Children: Working for Social Justice in the Primary School.* London: David Fulton Publishers.

Grisso, T. and Vierling, L. (1978) Minors' consent to treatment: A developmental perspective. *Professional Psychology 9,* 412–27.

Hardyment, C. (1984) *Dream Babies: Child Care from Locke to Spock.* Oxford: Oxford University Press.

Hart, R. (1992) *Children's Participation from Tokenism to Citizenship.* Paris: UNICEF.

Hart, R. (1997) *Children's Participation: The Theory and Practice of Involving Young Children in Community Development and Environmental Care.* London: Earthscan/UNESCO.

Hart, R. (1998) The developing capacities of children to participate. In V. Johnson, E. Ivan-Smith, G. Gordon, P. Pridmore and P. Scott (1998) *Stepping Forward: Children's and Young People's Participation in the Development Process.* London: Intermediate Technology.

Hendrick, H. (1990/97) Constructions and reconstructions of British childhood: An interpretive survey 1800 to the present. In A. James and A. Prout (eds) *Constructing and Reconstructing Childhood: Contemporary Issues of the Sociology of Childhood.* London: Falmer Press.

Herbert, E. and Moir, J. (1996) *Children and Special Educational Needs.* In C. Nutbrown (ed) (1996a) *Respectful Educators – Capable Learners: Children's Rights in Early Education.* London: Paul Chapman.

Highfield School (1997) *Changing our School: Promoting Positive Behaviour.* Edited by P. Alderson. Plymouth: Highfield School/London: Institute of Education.

Hillman, M., Adams, J. and Whiteleg, J. (1990) *One False Move: A Study of Children's Independent Mobility.* London: Policy Studies Institute.

Hodgkin, R. and Newell, P. (1996) *Effective Government Structures for Children.* London: Calouste Gulbenkian Foundation.

Hodgson, D. (1995) *Promoting Children's Rights in Practice.* London: NCVO.

Holden, C. and Clough, N. (1999) *Children as Citizens: Education for Participation.* London: Jessica Kingsley Publishers.

Holdigan, C. (2000) Discipline and normalisation in the nursery, the Foucauldian gaze. In H. Penn (ed) *Early Childhood Services: Theory, Policy and Practice.* Buckingham: Open University Press.

Howarth, R. and Hopscotch Asian Women's Centre (1997) *'If We Don't Play Now, When Can We?'* London: Hopscotch Asian Women's Centre.

Hurley, N. (1998) *Straight Talk: Working with Children and Young People in Groups.* York: Joseph Rowntree Foundation.

Hutchby, I. and Moran-Ellis, J. (eds) (1998) *Children and Social Competence: Arenas of Action.* London: Falmer.

Hutton, W. (1995) *The State We're In.* London: Jonathon Cape.

International Save the Children Alliance (1995) *UN Convention on the Rights of the Child Training Kit.* London: Save the Children.

Irwin, C. (1996) Samantha's wish. *Nursing Times 92,* 36, 30–31.

James, A. and Prout, A. (eds) (1990/97) *Constructing and Reconstructing Childhood: Contemporary Issues of the Sociology of Childhood.* London: Falmer Press.

Johnson, V., Hill, J. and Ivan-Smith, E. (1995) *Listening to Smaller Voices: Children in an Environment of Change.* Chard: ACTIONAID.

Johnson, V., Ivan-Smith, E., Gordon, G., Pridmore, P. and Scott, P. (1998) *Stepping Forward: Children and Young People's Participation in the Development Process.* London: Intermediate Technology.

Judd, D. (1995) *Give Sorrow Words: Working with a Dying Child.* Second edition. London: Whurr Publishers.

Kefyalew, F. (1996) The reality of child participation in research: Experience from a capacity-building programme. *Childhood 3*, 2, 203–14.

Kendrick, C., Culling, J., Oakhill, T. and Molt, M. (1986) Children's understanding of their illness and treatment within a paediatric oncology unit. *ACP Newsletter 8*, 2, 16–20.

Khan, S. (1997) *A Street Children's Research.* London: Save the Children/Dhaka: Chinnamul Shishu Kishore Sangstha.

Kiddle, C. (1999) *Traveller Children: A Voice for Themselves.* London: Jessica Kingsley Publishers.

Knight. A. (1998) *Valued or Forgotten? Independent Visitors and Disabled Young People.* London: National Children's Bureau.

Krementz, J. (1990) *How it Feels to Fight for your Life.* New York: Gollancz.

Kubler Ross, E. (1983) *On Children and Death.* London: Macmillan.

Laing, C. (1993) Statement at the launch of the National Playing Fields Association Report, 6 July, quoted in Lansdown, G. and Newell, P. (eds) (1994) *UK Agenda for Children.* London: Children's Rights Office.

Lane, J. (1999) *Action for Racial Equality in the Early Years: Understanding the Past, Thinking about the Present, Planning for the Future.* London: National Early Years Network.

Lansdown, G. (1995) *Taking Part, Children's Participation in Decision Making.* London: Institute for Public Policy Research.

Lansdown, G. and Newell, P. (eds) (1994) *UK Agenda for Children.* London: Children's Rights Office.

Leach, P. (1999) *The Physical Punishment of Children: Some Input from Recent Research.* London: NSPCC.

Lee, L. (1959) *Cider with Rosie.* London: Hogarth Press.

Leidloff, J. (1976) *The Continuum Concept.* London: Futura.

Levine, H. (1993) Context and scaffolding in developmental studies of mother-child problem-solving dyads. In S. Chaiklin and J. Lave (eds) *Understanding Practice.* Cambridge: Cambridge University Press.

Lewis, A. (1994) *Children's Understanding of Disability.* London: Routledge.

Llewellyn, N. (1993) The use of PCA for paediatric post-operative pain management. *Paediatric Nursing 5*, 12–15.

Lorenzo, R. (1992) *Too Little Time and Space for Childhood.* Florence: UNICEF.

Lukes, S. (1974) *Power.* Basingstoke: Macmillan.

MacCarthy, D. (1979) *The Under-Fives in Hospital.* London: National Association for the Welfare of Children in Hospital.

McNamara, S. and Moreton, G. (1993) *Teaching Special Needs in Mainstream Classes.* London: David Fulton.

McNamara, S. and Moreton, G. (1995) *Changing Behaviour.* London: David Fulton.

McNamara, S. and Moreton, G. (1997) *Understanding Differentiation.* London: David Fulton.

Madders, J. (1987) *Relax and be Happy: Techniques for 5–18 Year Olds.* London: Unwin.

Malaguzzi, L. (1998) Quoted in C. Edwards, I. Gandini and G. Forman (eds) The Hundred Languages of Children. London: Ablex. page xix–xxii.

Marlowe, J. (1997) Cries and whispers: Children are eager to show you their bleeding knees but not their broken hearts. *Guardian* 11 February.

Masson, J. and Winn, M. (1999) *Out of Hearing: Representing Children in Care Proceedings.* Chichester: Wiley.

Masson, J., Harrison, C. and Pavlovic, A. (1997) *Working with Children and 'Lost' Parents.* York: Joseph Rowntree Foundation.

Mayall, B. (1993) Keeping children healthy. *Social Science and Medicine 36,* 77–84.

Mayall, B. (1994a) *Negotiating Health: Primary School Children at Home and School.* London: Cassell.

Mayall, B. (1994b) *Children's Childhoods: Observed and Experienced.* London: Falmer Press.

Mayles, J. (1989) *Just Playing?* Buckingham: Open University Press.

Menzies Lyth, I. (1988) *Containing Anxiety in Institutions.* London: Free Association Books.

Mepani, B. and Emerson, S. (1998) *Report for the Steering Committee on Consulting with Children in East London.* London: Children's Discovery Centre: Save the Children.

Midgley, M. (1996) *Utopias, Dolphins and Computer: Problems of Philosophical Plumbing.* London: Routledge.

Miller, A. (1983) *Thou Shalt not be Aware: Society's Betrayal of the Child.* London: Pluto.

Miller, J. (1997) *Never too Young: How Young Children Can Take Responsibility and Make Decisions.* London: National Early Years Network/Save the Children.

Miller, J. (1998) But we didn't mean to do that! *Co-ordinate 67,* 5–6.

Miller, J. (1999) *Young Children as Decision-Makers: On Realising Children's Rights in England.* London: Save the Children.

Morris, J. (1998) *Don't Leave Us Out: Involving Disabled Children and Young People With Communication Impairments.* York: Joseph Rowntree Foundation.

Morris, S. (1999) Want a baby? Read this first. *The Times,* 12 March 99, p.21.

Morss, J. (1990) *The Biologising of Childhood.* Hillsdale NJ: Lawrence Erlbaum.

Morrow, V. (1994) Responsible children? In B. Mayall (ed) *Children's Childhoods Observed and Experienced.* London: Falmer.

Morrow, V. (1999) We get played like fools: Young people's accounts of community and institutional participation. *Health Education Authority Conference: Changing Families, Changing Communities.* London.

Mosley, J. (1993) *Turn Your School Around*. Wisbech: Learning Development Aids.

Moss, P. and Petrie, P. (1997) *Children's Services: Time for a New Agenda*. London: Institute of Education.

National Association of the Education of Young Children. (1992) *Code of Ethical Conduct*. Washington DC: NAYEC.

National Children's Bureau (1993) Guidelines for Research. London: NEB.

National Voluntary Council for Children's Play (1992) *A Charter for Children's Play*. London: National Children's Bureau.

Neustatter, A. (1998) Kids – what the papers say. *Guardian* 8 April.

Nevison, C. (1997) *'A Matter of Opinion' Research into Children and Young People's Participation Rights in the North East*. London: Save the Children.

NEYN (National Early Years Network/Redbridge Local Authority). (1998) *Developing Effective Consultation with Children and their Parents*. London: NEYN.

Newell, P. (1989) *Children Are People Too: The Case Against Physical Punishment*. London: Bedford Square Press.

Newson, C. (1995a) The patio projects. *Co-ordinate 45*, 10–11.

Newson, C. (1995b) Too much fun? *Co-ordinate 45*, 11.

Newson, J. and Newson, E. (1990) *The Extent of Parental Physical Punishment in the UK*. London: APPROACH.

Noyes, J. (1999) *The Voices and Choices of Children on Long-Term Ventilation*. London: Stationery Office.

Nutbrown, C. (ed) (1996a) *Respectful Educators – Capable Learners: Children's Rights in Early Education*. London: Paul Chapman.

Nutbrown, C. (1996b) Wide eyes and open minds. In C. Nutbrown (ed) *Respectful Educators – Capable Learners: Children's Rights in Early Education*. London: Paul Chapman. 44–55.

O'Neill, J. (1994) *The Missing Child in Liberal Theory: Towards a Covenant Theory of Family, Community, Welfare and the Civic State*. Toronto: University of Toronto Press.

O'Quigley, A. (1999) *Listening to Children and Representing their Best Interests*. York: Joseph Rowntree Foundation.

Parr, A. quoted in Ward, C. (1994) Opportunities for childhood in late twentieth century Britain. In B. Mayall (ed) *Children's Childhoods Observed and Experienced*. London: Falmer.

Parsons, C. (1996) Permanent exclusions from schools in England in the 1990s: Trends, causes and responses. *Children and Society 10*, 3, 177–86.

Pearce, J. (1998) *Centres for Curiosity and Imagination. When is a Museum not a Museum?* London: Calouste Gulbenkian Foundation.

PEG – Participation Education Group (1997) *School Can Seriously Damage Your Health: How Children Think School Affects and Deals with their Health*. Newcastle-upon-Tyne, PEG.

PEG (1998) *Newsletter, Celebration Edition*, May.

Penn, H. (1997a) *Comparing Nurseries: The Experiences of Children and Staff in Day Nurseries in Spain, Italy and the UK.* London: Paul Chapman.

Penn, H. (1997b) *Childcare As a Gendered Organisation. Research Report RR23.* London: DfEE.

Penn, H. (1998a) *A Review of Kindergarten Provision in Mongolia.* Report for the Ministry of Education and Culture, Mongolia.

Penn, H. (1998b) Children and childhood in the majority world. *Conference on Childhood: Relating Research to Policy.* London.

Penn, H. (1998c) You've got a friend. *Co-ordinate 66,* 5–6.

Piaget, J. (1924) *The Language and Thought of the Child.* London: Routledge.

Piaget, J. (1932) *The Moral Judgement of the Child.* London: Routledge.

Piaget, J. and Inhelder, B. (1956) *The Child's Conception of Space.* London: Routledge.

Pratt, B. and Loizos, P. (1992) *Choosing Research Methods: Data Collection for Development Workers.* Oxford: Oxfam.

Pritchard, M. (1991) *On Becoming Responsible.* Lawrence, Kansas: University of Kansas Press.

Pritchard, M. (1996) *Reasonable Children: Moral Education and Moral Learning.* Lawrence, Kansas: University of Kansas Press.

Purves, L. and Selleck, D. (1999) *Tuning Into Children.* (The handbook for the *Radio 4* series.) London: BBC.

Qualifications and Curriculum Authority (1998) *Education for Citizenship and Democracy* (The Crick Report). London: QCA.

Qvortrup, J., Bardy, M., Sgritta, G. and Wintersberger, H. (eds) (1994) *Childhood Matters: Social Theory, Practice and Politics.* Aldershot: Avebury.

Raban, K. (1987) Young children, guided imagery and religious education. *British Journal of Religious Education 10,* 1.

Ramsden, S. (1998) *Working with Children of Prisoners: A Resource for Teachers.* London: Save the Children.

Rankin, B. (1998) Curriculum development in Reggio Emilia. In C. Edwards, I. Gandini and G. Forman (eds) *The Hundred Languages of Children.* London: Ablex. pp.215–38.

Ransome, A. (1930) *Swallows and Amazons.* London: Jonathan Cape.

Richman, N. (1993) *Communicating with Children: Helping Children in Distress.* London: Save the Children.

Riihelda, M. (1996) *How do we Deal with Children's Questions?* Published PhD Thesis. Helsinki: STAKES.

Roberts, H. (1997) Children, inequalities and health: Socio-economic determinants of health. *British Medical Journal 314,* 1122–25.

Roberts, H. Smith, S. and Bryce, C. (1995) *Children at Risk? Safety as a Social Value.* Buckingham: Open University Press.

Robertson, J. and Robertson, J. (1989) *Separation and the Very Young.* London: Free Association Books.

Rose, N. (1990) *Governing the Soul: The Shaping of the Private Self.* London: Routledge.

Rosen, M. (1998) *The Penguin Book of Childhood.* Harmondsworth: Penguin.

Rowe, D. (1999) *The Business of School Councils.* London: The Citizenship Foundation.

Rutter, J. and Hyder, T. (1998) *Refugee Children in the Early Years: Issues for Policy-Makers and Providers.* London: Refugee Council and Save the Children.

Saunders, R. and Freeman, K. (1998) Children's neo-rhetorical participation in peer interactions. In I. Hutchby and J. Moran-Ellis (eds) *Children and Social Competence: Arenas of Action.* London: Falmer. pp.87–114.

Save the Children (1995) *Towards a Children's Agenda: New Challenges for Social Development.* London: Save the Children.

Save the Children (1997a) *Global Programme Strategy.* London: Save the Children.

Save the Children (1997b) *Childcare and Regeneration: Meeting the Needs of Parents and Children.* London: Save the Children.

Save the Children (1997c) *Learning From Experience: Participatory Approaches in SCF.* London: Save the Children.

Save the Children (n.d.) *Focus on Images.* London: Save the Children.

Save the Children (1998) *Staying Power.* London: Save the Children.

Save the Children (1999) *We Have Rights Okay!* London: Save the Children.

Save the Children/Kirklees Metropolitan Council (1996) *Children's Participation Pack: A Practical Guide for Playworkers.* London: Save the Children.

Selleck, D. and Griffin, S. (1996) Quality for the under-3s. In G. Pugh (ed) *Contemporary Issues in the Early Years: Working Collaboratively for Children.* London: National Children's Bureau.

Sgritta, G. (1997) Inconsistencies: Childhood on the economic and political agenda. *Childhood 4,* 4, 375–404.

Shamgar-Handelman, L. (1994) To whom does childhood belong? In J. Qvortop, M. Bardy, G. Sgritta and H. Wintersberger (eds) *Childhood Matters: Social Theory, Practice and Politics.* Aldershot: Avebury.

Sharman, C., Cross, W. and Vennis, D. (1995) *Observing Children: A Practical Guide, Case Studies.* London: Cassell.

Shier, H. (1995) *Article 31 Action Pack: Children's Rights and Children's Play.* PLAY-TRAIN, Birmingham, England.

Siegal, M. (1997) *Knowing Children: Experiments in Conversation and Cognition.* Hove: Lawrence Erlbaum Associates.

Siraj-Blatchford, I. (1996) *Language, Cultures and Difference: Challenging Inequalities and Promoting Respect.* In C. Nutbrown (ed) (1996a) *Respectful Educators – Capable Learners: Children's Rights in Early Education.* London: Paul Chapman. pp.23–33.

Skeat, W. (1983) *Concise Etymological Dictionary of the English Language.* Oxford: Oxford University Press.

Smith, C. (1998) Children with 'special rights'. In C. Edwards, I. Gandini and G. Forman (eds) *The Hundred Languages of Children.* London: Ablex. pp.199–214.

Smith, F. (1998) Child-centred after school and holiday child care. *Report to ESRC Children 5–16 Programme Meeting.* Manchester.

Smith, M. (1995) A community study of physical violence to children in the home and associated variables. *Fifth European Conference, International Society for the Prevention of Child Abuse and Neglect.* Oslo.

Smith, M. (1998) Paper on Children's views about violence. *Report to ESRC Children 5–16 Programme Meeting.* Manchester.

Snowden, B. (1996) New reproductive technologies: Children's rights and the Human Fertilisation and Embryology Act. In M. John (ed) *Children in Our Charge: The Child's Rights to Resources.* London: Jessica Kingsley Publishers.

Solberg, A. (1990/97) Negotiating childhood. In A. James and A. Prout (eds) *Constructing and Reconstructing Childhood: Contemporary Issues of the Sociology of Childhood.* London: Falmer Press.

Solberg, A. (1993) The social construction of childhood. In B. Mayall (ed) *Family Life and Social Control: Report of Child Study Group Seminar.* London: Social Science Research Unit.

Stainton-Rogers, R. and Stainton-Rogers, W. (1992) *Stories of Childhood: Shifting Agendas in Child Concern.* Hemel Hempstead: Harvester.

Stern, D. (1990) *Diary of a Baby.* New York: Basic Books.

Stone, M. (1995) *Don't Just Do Something, Sit There: Developing Children's Spiritual Awareness.* Norwich: Religious and Moral Education Press.

Stoppard, M. (1998) *The New Parent.* London: Dorling Kindersley.

Strandell, H. (2000) What is the use of children's play: Preparation or social participation? In H. Penn (ed) *Early Childhood Services: Theory, Policy and Practice.* Buckingham: Open University Press.

Thomas, N. (1998) Finding a voice for a 'muted group': Children's involvement in decision-making when they are 'looked after' in middle childhood. Paper to *Children and Social Exclusion Conference.* Hull.

Thornborrow, J. (1998) Children's participation in the discourse of children's television. In I. Hutchby and J. Moran-Ellis (eds) *Children and Social Competence: Arenas of Action.* London: Falmer. 134–154.

Tizard, B. and Hughes, M. (1984) *Young Children Learning.* London: Faber.

Treseder, P. (1997) *Empowering Children and Young People: A Training Manual for Promoting Involvement in Decision-Making.* London: Save the Children/Children's Rights Office.

Trevarthen, C. (1999) Quoted in L. Purves and D. Selleck. *Tuning into Children.* London: BBC.

United Nations (1989) *Convention on the Rights of the Child.* Geneva: UN.

United Nations Committee on the Rights of the Child (1995) *Concluding Observation of the Committee on the Rights of the Child: UK of Great Britain and Northern Ireland. Consideration of Reports Submitted by States Parties under Article 44 of the Convention.* Geneva: UN.

Verhellen, E. (1994) *Convention on the Rights of the Child: Background, Motivation, Strategies, Main Themes.* Leuven: Garant.

Ward, L. (1997) *Seen and Heard: Involving Disabled Children and Young People in Research and Development Projects.* York: Joseph Rowntree Foundation.

Wellard, S., Tearse, M. and West, A. (1997) *All Together Now: Community Participation for Children and Young People.* London: Save the Children.

West, A. (1995) *'You are on Your Own': Young People's Research on Leaving Care.* London: Save the Children.

Whaley, K. and Rubenstein, T. (1994) How toddlers 'do' friendship. *Journal of Social and Personal Responsibility 11,* 23, 383–400.

Whalley, M. (1992) Working as a team in G. Pugh (ed) *Contemporary Issues in the Early Years.* London: Paul Chapman/Early Years.

Whalley, M. (1998) Excellence in the early years. Paper presented to a Conference at Pen Green, Corby

White, B. (1996) Globalisation and the child labour problem. *Journal of International Development 8,* 6, 829–39.

Wilkinson, R. (1994) *Unfair Shares: The Effects of Widening Income Differences on the Welfare of the Young.* Barkingside: Barnardo's.

Willow, C. (1996) *Children's Rights and Participation in Residential Care.* London: NCB.

Willow, C. (1997) *Hear! Hear! Promoting Children and Young People's Democratic Participation in Local Government.* London: Local Government Information Unit.

Willow, C. and Hyder, T. (1998) *It Hurts You Inside: Children Talk About Smacking.* London: National Children's Bureau/Save the Children.

Wipfler, P. (1990) *Listening to Children: Playlistening.* Palo Alto CA: Parents Leadership Institute.

Woodhead, M. (1990/1997) Psychology and the cultural construction of children's needs. In A. James and A. Prout (eds) *Constructing and Reconstructing Childhood: Contemporary Issues of the Sociology of Childhood.* London: Falmer Press.

Woodhead, M. (1998) Understanding child development in the context of children's rights. In C. Cunninghame (ed) *Realising Children's Rights.* London: Save the Children.

Woodhead, M. (1999) Reconstructing Developmental Psychology – some first steps. *Children and Society 13,* 3–19.

Resources

Further details about work with young children are available from these organisations.

Children's Legal Centre
University of Essex
Wivenhoe Park
Colchester
Essex CO4 3SQ
01206 873 820
www2.essex.ac.uk/clc

Children's Rights International Network
Centre for Europe's Children
University of Glasgow
Scotland
www.crin.org

Children's Rights Office
City Road
London EC1V 1LJ
020 7278 8222
www.cro.org.uk

Daycare Trust
Shoreditch Town Hall Annexe
380 Old Street
London EC1V 9LT
020 7739 2866
www.daycaretrust.org.uk

EPOCH
End Physical Punishment of Children
77 Holloway Road
London N7 8JZ
020 7700 0627

National Children's Bureau
8 Wakely Street
London EC1V 7QE
020 7843 6000
www.ncb.org.uk

National Early Years Network
77 Holloway Road
London N7 8JZ
020 7607 9573

Save the Children Centre for Young Children's Rights
356 Holloway Road
London N7 6PA
020 7700 8127
www.savethechildren.org.uk

Subject Index

Author Index